The World, the Flesh and the Si

The World, the Flesh and the Subject

Continental Themes in Philosophy of Mind and Body

Paul Gilbert and Kathleen Lennon

Edinburgh University Press

© Paul Gilbert and Kathleen Lennon, 2005

Edinburgh University Press
22 George Square, Edinburgh

Typeset in Sabon
by Koinonia, Bury, and
printed and bound in Great Britain
by MPG Books Ltd, Bodmin, Cornwall

A CIP record for this book is available from the British Library

ISBN 0 7486 1498 2 (hardback)
ISBN 0 7486 1499 0 (paperback)

The right of Paul Gilbert and Kathleen Lennon
to be identified as authors of this work
has been asserted in accordance with
the Copyright, Designs and Patents Act 1988.

Contents

Preface

In an earlier work, *Philosophy of Mind* (with Stephen Burwood, UCL Press, 1998), we offered an introduction to contemporary Anglo-American approaches to the subject and suggested a critique of them for their neglect of the lived body and our engagement with the world. In this book we carry forward this project by discussing the topics that have proved most problematic for these approaches. They remain problematic, we believe, partly because of a disregard for the insights of Continental philosophers which can be brought to bear upon them. We aim to make these insights accessible and to bring them into dialogue with the standard treatments.

Like our earlier book, this owes its origins to our MA in the Philosophy of Mind and Body at Hull University. We would like to thank past students on this course, doctoral students in Philosophy, and our other colleagues here for stimulation and illumination. We also thank Edinburgh University Press's editor, Jackie Jones, our copy-editor, Peter Andrews, and the Philosophy Secretaries for all their help.

An earlier version of Chapter 3 by Kathleen Lennon appeared as 'Imaginary Bodies and Worlds' in *Inquiry* vol. 47 (2004) pp. 107–22, and we thank the Editor and publishers, Taylor & Francis AS (www.tandf.no/inquiry) for permission to reproduce some material here.

Introduction

In a recent TV drama one of the characters falls in love with another. 'It's only chemicals,' his friend assures him, but when the friend finds himself in the same position he is unable to take the same view of his own situation. It would be a caricature to represent the dominant paradigm in contemporary Anglo-American philosophy of mind as holding of all our psychological states, 'It's only chemicals.' Yet this paradigm – functionalism – does hold that each of them is, in fact, a physiological state, but one individuated in terms of its function in mediating between sensory inputs and behavioural outputs. It is *only* that, because there is no mysterious mental extra of the sort that a discredited dualism would postulate. Creditable as this rejection of dualism may be, however, it nonetheless jettisons along with it the very feature that most made it plausible, namely, the role of psychological states in providing *our reasons* for acting as we do. And this is precisely what the 'It's only chemicals' style of explanation fails to acknowledge. Yet the character who falls in love does have a reason for his actions, and one we can all understand, but one which the identification of his condition with a functional state does nothing to illuminate.

The functionalist paradigm is not, of course, the only current in contemporary Anglo-American philosophy of mind, and there are influential approaches which do seek to emphasise the reason-giving role of psychological explanation. For all that, it is the dominant one because it sees philosophy as working hand in hand with empirical psychology, neurophysiology and computer science to account for mental functioning as part of the natural world that science investigates, and thus it helps itself to the prestige that accrues to scientific investigation. It aims to resolve the traditional problem of relating mind and body by taking over the scientific conception of the body as a mechanism whose internal workings must, ultimately, be what explain behaviour.

Yet this model of explanation inevitably creates two problems. First, it fails to show how that we act as we do depends on the way we relate to the world. For the functional state which supposedly explains our acts is an internal state which could, in principle, be the same whatever the world outside was like. Yet it is our actions in the world that need explaining, and this requires showing how we relate to that world and what its significance for us is. Secondly, we can seemingly imagine creatures with the same functional states as we have but lacking the same subjective character as our experiences have. Yet it is just this character – the way love *feels*, for instance – that often gives us the reasons that explain our acts. These two problems – of intentionality and of consciousness respectively – are those that continue to exercise functionalists and to shape the research programme of the dominant paradigm. Arguably, however, given the model of explanation and explanatory states it works with, they are insoluble.

This book, by contrast, aims to develop an alternative which starts out from the very feature the dominant paradigm most neglects – the way psychological states explain behaviour by showing how they provide our reasons for acting as we do. Key to this, we shall maintain, is that reporting these states involves revealing an aspect of the agent's perspective upon the world. What makes them reasons for an action is the fact that from this perspective that course of action is the appropriate thing to do. We understand her action just because we grasp that, and to grasp that involves imaginatively sharing her perspective. We have to be the same sort of creature as she is to do this. But this is not because the inner workings of our brains replicate those of hers, as some functionalists contend. It is because, allowing for individual differences, things in the world have the same sort of significance for us as they do for her. Since this relation is reflexive the project of psychological explanation is, on this model, one of *mutual* intelligibility; and this marks it out as dramatically different from scientific explanation, where the object of study need have no affinity with its observer. But it is this feature that made the 'It's only chemicals' style of explanation impossible to apply to ourselves and, for that reason, deeply unsatisfying.

The alternative paradigm we develop is, then, hermeneutic, in aiming to make our actions intelligible to us, and phenomenological, in doing so by revealing how the world presents itself to us when we so act. Since it is principally Continental philosophers who have adopted this approach it is these that we mainly draw upon in trying to illustrate how it sheds light on some principal psychological concepts: perception, sensation, imagination, desire, emotion and agency. In pursuit of such illumination we make use not only of phenomenological and hermeneutic thought, but also of strands of psychoanalytic, post-structuralist and feminist writings. What serves as an argument for our alternative is a claim for its superior fecundity in elucidating just such concepts, by comparison with the dominant paradigm. But a judgement as to that must be left to the reader.

What will be objected to, however, will be the apparent departure from a naturalistic psychology that the alternative explanatory paradigm represents. This, we shall try to show, is an illusion. For we shall aim to demonstrate the way in which psychological phenomena are intimately related to the body. In this work philosophy of mind and philosophy of body are intertwined. The body as it is conceived here, however, is not that presented to us by physical science, but the body as it is encountered in ordinary life. This is one element – the flesh – among the three represented in our title. We shall also aim to show how embodied agents are related to the world in which they act, as, we suggested a moment ago, the functionalist paradigm cannot. But this relationship too is a natural one, in which the significance of things in the world ultimately derives from their relevance to us as living and breathing creatures, not as mysterious spiritual substances.

This brings us to the third element, the subject, whose place in the world as the centre of an embodied perspective upon it again needs to be treated naturalistically. We therefore aim to bring out, for example, the connection between the way things in the world are experienced and the manner in which our bodies are affected by and react to them. Again the treatment is a phenomenological one, of a sort unavailable to functionalism. In a final chapter we also relate the constitution of the subject to her interactions with other human beings and to the grounding of mutual intelligibility which these provide.

The overall result of bringing the three elements of the title into play in discussing the book's topics is not, unlike functionalism, a *theory*. It exemplifies an alternative paradigm and one, no doubt, with various theoretical presuppositions. Where the presuppositions of the different Continental philosophers we draw upon seem to come into conflict we try to resolve it. But, to repeat, we offer no general defence of our approach. We do, however, offer a more detailed account of the various psychological concepts we investigate than recent general works in philosophy of mind tend to provide. It is these, we suggest, that provide the principal interest of this area of study, and they do so because of their role in our understanding of ourselves and others. The approach we adopt is intended, in a modest way, to further that understanding, as no 'It's only chemicals' type of explanation can.

The Character of Experience

The Problem of Experience

For much of the last century philosophy of mind has been dominated by the attempt to give an account of mental states that does not have recourse to the Cartesian picture of them as essentially private, in the sense of being only providentially connected with the behaviour through which they are expressed. The states that have seemed particularly recalcitrant to such attempts are our experiences in perception and bodily sensation; for these paradigmatically have a subjective character – a something it is like to have them, as Thomas Nagel puts it[1] – that apparently eludes explanation in terms of the bodily processes that produce behaviour. Thus for Anglo-American analytic philosophy the key puzzle in the mind/body problem is how to explain why these processes should be accompanied by mental states with their distinctive subjective characters. And it is key partly because of the significance such states have in the Anglo-American empiricist tradition; namely, as the states which are basic in relating their subject to the world that perception reveals.

Recent analytic philosophy has attempted to solve the puzzle by suggesting systems in the brain which would not function as they do without its possessor having sensations with the subjective character they do. But all such suggestions are met, rightly or wrongly, with the response that we can imagine these systems so functioning to produce behaviour without the required experiences. In a similar vein, the account that is offered of how visual sensations, for example, are involved in our perception of the world describes the sorts of process whereby information from the world is transmitted to a subject, to be utilised in behaviour. Again an analogous response may be forthcoming: how can the *look* of a thing, thought of in terms of the subjective character of how it appears, be essential to such an information-receiving

process? Yet, conversely, what is typically regarded as a separate epistemological problem asks how mere visual sensations of this character
can vouchsafe knowledge of the external world, which perception
ostensibly provides – how, in other words, can they really serve to relate
us to the world?

Continental philosophy, too, has faced the same problem of providing an alternative to the Cartesian picture of experience, but its
approach has been a very different one, as this chapter will try to show.
The reasons for this are threefold. First, the notion of the body and the
behaviour it manifests is not left unscrutinised, as in the analytic
tradition, but is itself subjected to investigation as one of the factors
which give rise to the problem. Second, and, as we shall see, relatedly,
the notion of the subject of experience, for whom sensations have a
certain character, is also interrogated, rather than being taken for
granted. In particular, subjectivity is typically related to a subject's life,
so that it is as lived experience that sensations need to be understood.
Third, the kind of understanding sought is characteristically first-
personal, so that what is offered is an account that attempts to clarify
why someone who has the experiences she does should find herself
acting as she does and vice versa. This hermeneutic approach is related
to the second point, for to understand something from the point of view
of the subject is to understand it as it figures in her life. It has, however,
an important consequence: the act of imagining we are invited to make
in envisaging behaviour disconnected from the subjective character of
experience is now to be undertaken from the point of view of the
subject, rather than from an observer's standpoint. From the former
position it is far less clear that this disconnection is imaginable, though
why not is yet to be clarified. There is a further important upshot of the
foregoing considerations. It is that the 'psychological' and 'epistemological' questions, treated separately in analytic philosophy, may be
considered together within the Continental tradition. That is to say, the
question of why an experience that elicits certain behaviour has the
subjective character it does can be answered by showing how it can
provide knowledge of the world in virtue of having that character. Or,
to put the point differently, the two questions can be resolved together
by presenting the subjective character of the experience as an aspect of
the way the world appears to an agent engaging with it. And these
questions can be answered together because from the point of view of
the agent it is the way the world is that is of cardinal importance, so that
what it is like for her to experience it as she does needs to be understood
in terms of the way this reveals the world as being.

This is not, of course, to say that there has not been within the analytic tradition any scrutiny of the idea of experiences as they occur in perception or bodily sensation. There has, in particular, been considerable discussion of what constitutes the so-called 'contents of consciousness' – a phrase which, as we shall see, is dangerously apt to mislead, however metaphorical its force is taken to be. In this connection anti-Cartesian philosophers of a Wittgensteinian stamp have been anxious to exorcise one or other version of the 'myth of the given'[2] – the notion that the content of consciousness is something presented to one in sensation, which then becomes the material, as it were, for one's thoughts about one's body or the world beyond it. Wittgenstein's own attack stems from the *redundancy* of any such privately presented contents in grounding judgments about our sensations; whatever role reference to sensations plays in our talk about ourselves or the world, it cannot be explained in terms of anything supposedly given to consciousness, for our talk could go on in the same way whatever was so given or in the absence of it. This is not the place to spell out this familiar 'private language argument'.[3] Its corollary for Wittgenstein was that our sensation avowals, spoken or unspoken, were not reports of anything *known* to their subjects, still less known only to them, but were rather to be construed as replacements for more primitive behavioural responses, like 'ouch!' let out when in pain. But while this suggestion certainly presupposes embodied subjects it does little to illuminate why pains should feel the way they do, if only because I cannot readily regard my *own* thought absorbed by pain as no more than a sophisticated silent scream.

The myth of the given is, however, not the only problem with the picture of contents of consciousness. The myth certainly conveys a common view of what happens in perception, namely that I am presented with an inner object that has certain properties – being white, round and moving fast across my visual field, say – on the basis of which I discern a football. This is, though, phenomenologically implausible: I just notice, assuming I am right about it, a football, and the features of the way it appears strike me, if they strike me at all, only later. But we need not tell this implausible story to encounter a related conception of content that again fails to illuminate the subjective character of experience. It is one that distinguishes the intentional, or as it is sometimes put the representational, content from the phenomenal or sensational. The intentional object of a psychological state is, of course, that item in the world[4] towards which it is directed, as when it really is a football I discern. The phenomenal or sensational properties of the state are those supposedly non-intentional ones that hold, for example, of my visual field when the ball presents a bigger image as it gets closer, although it does not look as if it is growing larger. But even to *raise* the question of whether there are these additional properties that cannot be explained in intentional terms is to be misled by talk of 'representations' and 'images' into supposing that there is something presented to the senses, whether or not regarded as the 'given', such that there is a sense in which consciousness literally has *contents* – items depending upon it for their existence.

Now we have only to turn, for example, to Sartre to see this conception, so persistent in Anglo-American philosophy, repudiated. And in repudiating it Sartre is, in effect, only reinforcing a theme taken for granted on the Continent since Franz Brentano formulated it in the late nineteenth century,[5] namely, that the mark of the mental is precisely its intentionality – its directedness towards things in the world – rather than, as on the Cartesian model, consciousness, which itself needs construing in intentional terms. Sartre notes:

> All consciousness is consciousness *of* something. This definition of conscious-ness can be taken in two very distinct senses: either we understand by this that consciousness is constitutive of the being of its object, or it means that consciousness in its inmost nature is a relation to a transcendent being. But the first interpretation destroys itself: to be conscious *of* something is to be confronted with a concrete and full presence which *is not* consciousness.[6]

'Appearances', as Sartre somewhat confusingly calls the objects of consciousness, are the actual things in the world which we perceive: 'the being of an existent is exactly what it *appears*'.[7] Appearances are not mind-dependent representations or images of things independent of the mind, which are the causes of impressions confined to consciousness, for 'the being of the phenomenon can on no account act upon consciousness'.[8] Or, to put the point differently, what it is like to have particular visual experiences is not to be explained in terms of causal processes initiated by external objects and culminating in properties of consciousness. Lacking any contents, consciousness is not an entity, Sartre holds, which could be causally affected. What it is like to experience something in the world is rather to be elucidated in terms of our embodied relation to it.

Indeed, Sartre insists that the subject of consciousness, the ego, is not 'in consciousness: it is outside, *in the world*. It is a being of the world, like the ego of another.'[9] Its fundamental mode of existence is activity in the world, which yields what Sartre calls 'pre-reflective' consciousness, rather than the Cartesian 'reflective' consciousness involved in surveying supposed mental contents. The latter view results from embracing what Sartre anathematises as 'the primacy of knowledge'[10] –

the idea that our fundamental relation to the world is a cognitive one. Instead, Sartre holds that cognitive relations to the world consist primarily in acting upon it. His own example is that of coming to know there are a dozen cigarettes in a case by counting them, an activity of which I need not be reflectively aware but which requires a certain direction of attention upon the world. 'The point of view of pure knowledge', he later writes, 'is contradictory; there is only the point of view of *engaged* knowledge. This amounts to saying that knowledge and action are only two aspects of an original concrete relation.'[11] To grasp the basis for this kind of claim, fundamental not only to Sartre's non-Cartesian account of experience but to that of much subsequent Continental philosophy, whatever its differences with him, we need to turn to his mentor, Martin Heidegger, for Sartre explicitly associates his account of consciousness with Heidegger's conception of *Dasein* and its *Being-in-the-World*.[12]

Living in the World

Heidegger's breakthrough in resisting the Cartesian picture of experience, still influential in the problematic of analytic philosophy, was twofold. Both are implicit in the curious German word Heidegger chooses to refer to us as people – *Dasein* – literally 'being-there' and normally used for the existence of people, rather than of a person. Heidegger, however, exploits the two components of the word to bring out what he regards as essential to being a person: first, that a person is *there* – located in a world, since 'to say that in existing, Dasein is its "there", is equivalent to saying that the world is "there"; its *Being-there* is "Being-in"';[13] and second, that one's primary relation to the world is one of *existing* in it, for '*the essence of Dasein lies in its existence*'.[14] Each of these features stands in flat contradiction to those assumed in the Cartesian picture, which, first, prescinds from our location in a world in order to ask intelligibly how our experiences might yield knowledge of that world and, second, therefore regards consciousness, construed as the having of such thoughts and experiences, as the essential aspect of our subjectivity.

Heidegger starts, in fact, by asking what it is like to live in the world we do, and only derivatively what it is like to have the experiences viewed in analytic philosophy as palmary of subjective character. 'Not', says Heidegger, 'until the nature of this Being has been determined can we grasp the kind of Being which belongs to *cogitationes*',[15] that is, to such experiences. He goes on to investigate what constitutes *Dasein*'s 'Being-in-the-world', as exemplified in 'knowing the world', but he

immediately rejects the subject/object picture of observational knowledge. If this is to be possible, he asserts challengingly,

> [T]here must first be a *deficiency* in our having-to-do with the world
> concernfully. When concern holds back from any kind of producing, manipu-
> lating, and the like, it puts itself into what is now the sole remaining mode of
> Being-in … This kind of Being towards the world is one which lets us encounter
> entities within-the-world purely in the *way they look* … just that.[16]

Later Heidegger makes a similar point:

> What we 'first' hear is never noises or complexes of sounds, but the creaking
> wagon, the motor-cycle … It requires an artificial and complicated frame of
> mind to 'hear' a 'pure noise'. The fact that motor-cycles and wagons are what
> we proximally hear is the phenomenal evidence that in every case *Dasein*, as
> Being-in-the-world, already dwells *alongside* what is ready-to-hand within-the-
> world; it certainly does not dwell proximally alongside 'sensations'; nor would
> it first have to give shape to the swirl of sensations to provide the springboard
> from which the subject leaps off and finally arrives at a 'world'.[17]

He is not merely saying here that our perceptual states are already
charged with their intentional objects – motor-cycle, wagon and so on –
which cannot be somehow constructed out of their 'sensational' properties. He is saying that where the motor-cycles or the wagon are
playing their usual role in our lives, as bits of equipment being used for
some human purpose, we do not hear them *as* noises with distinctive
auditory characteristics. Indeed, if I am personally concerned with them
– awaiting the wagon's arrival, say, I just recognise the wagon by its
sound, for instance, without having any appreciation of what that
distinctive sound is, for this would require 'an artificial and complicated
frame of mind'.

Conversely the world of equipment, of things ready-to-hand, as
Heidegger calls them, cannot be grasped by observation. 'No matter
how sharply we *look* at the 'outward appearance' of Things in whatever
form this takes, we cannot discover anything ready-to-hand.'[18] What is
needed is a quite different kind of 'sight' which Heidegger terms
'circumspection', and which is manifest in our using things appropriately,
as, for example, when we turn the door knob to enter a room through
the door. We do not, of course, pass through doorways blindly, but
neither do we need to attend to what we are doing or to the things
involved in our doing them. Our commerce with these things is
unmediated by such experiences. It is a central theme of Heidegger's
that this kind of activity is fundamental to our life in the world. This
should not be misunderstood. Heidegger never intended, as he wrote
elsewhere, 'to assert … that the essence of man consists in his wielding a

spoon and fork and riding on the streetcar'.[19] And he was not simply
reversing the priorities of practical and theoretical knowledge. Rather
he uses activities made possible by practical knowledge to exemplify the
concern which underlies all knowledge: 'the kind of dealing which is
closest to us ... is not a bare perceptual cognition, but rather that kind
of concern which manipulates things and puts them to use: and this has
its own kind of "knowledge"'.[20] This kind of knowledge is, in a certain
sense, not based upon *perceptual* experiences at all, although it does, of
course, require the use of our senses.

Such experiences occur, Heidegger maintains, in special circumstances.
In particular, as noted earlier, it is when there is some 'deficiency' in our
dealings with the world. In all the dealings with which we concern
ourselves we care about the outcomes and this, Heidegger stresses, is an
essential feature of *Dasein*, because, as he famously announces, it is an
entity for whom its being is an issue[21] – we cannot view our existence in
the world indifferently. But the unimpeded employment of equipment
which exemplifies concernful dealings can break down or be suspended.
Heidegger considers each to constitute a 'deficiency'. In the former case
something is, for example, missing though needed for one's task – the
door knob is off the door, say. The door – a thing normally ready-to-
hand in the sense of usable for our purposes – now becomes, as
Heidegger puts it, 'obtrusive' to the extent that 'it seems to lose its
character of readiness-to-hand' and 'reveals itself as something just
present-at-hand and no more, without the thing that is missing. The
helpless way in which we stand before it is a deficient mode of concern.'[22]
Here what it is like to suddenly see the door just as a thing in front of
one, stems from one's impotence before it, one's incapacity to move
through the portal, which brings into focus its flat, blank face. It is
features of the experience such as this that make the visual sensation
what it is; but they are features from one's life in the world, not one's
life prior to it.

The other sort of situation is, Heidegger seems to suggest, even more
deficient in making the world available for our concernful dealings with
it. 'Leaving undone, neglecting, renouncing, taking a rest', he writes 'are
ways of concern; but these are all *deficient* modes, in which the
possibilities of concern are kept to a "bare minimum"'.[23] For example,
when we take a rest 'there is no longer anything ready to hand which we
must concern ourselves with bringing close', so that circumspection
'tends away from what is most closely ready-to-hand, and into a far and
alien world. Care becomes concern with the possibilities of seeing the
"world" merely as it *looks* while one tarries and takes a rest.' Heidegger
calls this attitude 'curiosity' which 'concerns itself with seeing, not in

order to understand what is seen ... but *just* in order to see'.[24] Here
Heidegger invites us to reflect upon what it is like to have a certain type
of experience and to see how this is a feature of the way the world
appears to us in such an experience. This sort of attention to the look of
things is precisely one that declines to see them as items of current use,
and it thus removes its subject from her usual relation to the world as
exemplified in using the things in it. It is scarcely surprising, then, that
concentration on such experiences should obscure that primary relation.
What treating them as somehow primitive overlooks, however, is the
fact that they *presuppose* our usual concerns with the world in virtue of
our desire to minimise them, which is an essential feature of the mode of
attention they require, and thus of what it is like to have these
experiences.

There is a way in which experiences like these are, indeed, *not* cases
of what Heidegger calls 'Dasein's "sight"',[25] for such sight as is manifest
in circumspection involves understanding its objects, that is, grasping
their significance for one, which is just what experiences only of the
look of a thing fail to yield. For this reason Heidegger is able to claim
that 'by showing how all sight is grounded primarily in understanding
... we have deprived pure intuition of its priority',[26] and, of course, he
includes here as examples of 'sight' all of the senses. A further consequence is that the prioritisation of objects as merely present-at-hand,
that is, as simply such and such spatial and material entities, is also
repudiated, because, as we have seen, it is only in experiences that deviate
from the norm in various ways that they present this appearance.

What overall account can we derive, then, from Heidegger's treatment of experience? While, as a phenomenologist, he shares the view
that our experiences are to be characterised in terms of the intentional
objects towards which they are directed, it is equally clear that he does
not see their character as exhausted by this fact. It is equally the door
that I see when I pass through it effortlessly and when it becomes
'obtrusive' because I cannot. Similarly it is not necessarily the case that I
see something more when I concern myself only with the look of the
thing than when I treat it as serving some present purpose. Rather,
because the circumstances in which I see the same things are different,
my experience is different too, and this shows up in the different
reactions I have. But what is the nature of this difference in my experience, if not in different intentional objects on the one hand or, on some
difference in the intrinsic qualities of the experiences – in the way they
feel, so to speak, construed as such a difference – on the other?

The difference does not lie in different intentional objects because the
beliefs about the situation with which the different experiences provide

one may be the same. That an object is encountered now as something ready-to-hand and now as merely present-at-hand is not necessarily to encounter it under aspects that yield different beliefs about it. Of course it may be so, as when I form no belief as to the use of an unfamiliar object, on the one hand, or few beliefs about the precise shape, size and so forth of a familiar one, on the other. But none of that is necessary to the difference with which we are concerned. Instead, the same belief as to what is confronted – that it is a door of a certain sort, say – may be grounded in different sorts of experience. In the one case, it is grounded in unimpeded actions of opening and passing through the door; in another, in stopping and looking. We grasp the character of each of these different sorts of experience through seeing how each can ground the same belief about a door. No doubt the difference between them comes out too in the different attitudes for which they also provide a reason: in the former case, for a kind of easy indifference; in the latter, for an interest, either troubled or merely curious depending upon my concerns and how the door affects them. What I want to do, in the light of the different experiences, differs in each case, and we would not have grasped the character of the experiences properly unless we could see why this was so. We would not, for example, grasp what simply opening and passing through a door was like if we thought it gave us a reason to be exasperated by the door and to want to kick it.

Both the different modes of engagement we have with the world (including the sorts of detachment from it that are possible) and the different positions we occupy in some mode of engagement – success, check, failure – alter our perspective upon the world and hence the character of our experience. Heidegger's claim, however, is that what is common to these perspectives is that they are all occupied precisely by an agent engaged with the world, so that the world she encounters, as manifest in the intentional objects of her experience, is given in terms of this engagement. This is not to say that she constructs her world *ab initio*. She is, Heidegger stresses, 'thrown'[27] into it with its contents already replete with significance for her. But they are significant because of their salience to the projects she engages with, be they matters of life and death, as some will inevitably be, with the anxiety which that involves, or merely quite trivial concerns, to be conducted light-heartedly.

Such different modes of engagement colour our experiences differently: a narrow path with a sheer drop on one side feels very different from one through green fields, say, and this is reflected in the different way in which we walk along them, even at points at which what is within our field of vision is the same (it is, after all, natural to avert one's gaze from the void and focus on the path alone). It is not just that feelings of anxiety accompany the experience in the one case but not the other. The ways the paths appear differ, though not in ways that can be captured in terms of reasons for different beliefs. But how things appear, in this sense what it is like to experience them, always depends, Heidegger insists, on the significance they have for us in our existence in a world of such things.

This general account has implications for the way Heidegger views the human body, for, though it is not met with in space in the way that other items present-at-hand can be, it cannot be assumed to be just another such entity, as Descartes and, following in his theoretical footsteps, most analytic philosophers who pose the mind/body problem have taken it to be. Heidegger acknowledges that *Dasein*'s '"bodily nature" hides a whole problematic of its own',[28] but disclaims any discussion of it in *Being and Time*. We can get some clue to his conception, however, not only from his repeated rejection[29] of the Cartesian-inspired picture of human beings as subjects of experience somehow linked to physical organisms but also from his account of the way being *in* the world is not a spatial relation, in the ordinary sense. It is, Heidegger asserts, 'because Dasein is "spiritual", *and only because of this* [that] it can be spatial in a way which remains essentially impossible for any extended corporeal Thing'. *Dasein* does not just 'fill up a bit of space', as such things do: it 'makes room for itself',[30] and this requires the sort of capacity to deal with one's environment that we have discussed earlier, a capacity inconceivable without the concern that Heidegger here ironically dubs 'spiritual'.

The sort of thing Heidegger has in mind by the body making room for itself is exemplified in such actions as reaching and grasping for something – the door knob, say – in which we have, entirely without calculation, successfully changed the space our bodies fill up in order to accomplish some simple task. In these situations, says Heidegger, the exact knowledge of space on which we depend 'remains blind'.[31] But this is not because we are somehow unconsciously computing distances from the position of our body conceived in terms of its physical spatial co-ordinates. We are not related to our own bodies like this because, while we place them in relation to their distance from other things, those distances are measured, not in terms of physical spatiality, but of what is close or far in terms of the ease of accomplishing the actions relevant to our situation. So, notes Heidegger,

> the street ... one feels ... at every step as one walks ... is seemingly the closest ... of all that is ready-to-hand, and it slides itself, as it were, along certain portions of one's body – the soles of one's feet. And yet it is farther remote than the acquaintance whom one encounters ... at ... twenty paces.[32]

It is, Heidegger comments, circumspective concern that determines what counts as close, that is, what one is currently concerning oneself with – greeting an acquaintance, say – for one's walking can, so to speak, take care of itself.

It is this kind of closeness that Heidegger has in mind when he remarks that 'no behaviour in which one feels one's way by touch can be "completed" unless what can thus be felt has "closeness" of a very special kind'.[33] He is here rejecting Descartes's idea that what is revealed by the sense of touch is that another material body like one's own is not giving up its place. But resistance to touch, Heidegger suggests, can only be felt as it is because things in the world matter to us, as they do: without that, 'resistance itself would remain essentially undiscovered'.[34] What it is like to encounter such a resistance when one reaches out and touches something depends upon how it matters. When I walk down the street it offers, of course, resistance to the soles of my feet, yet there is, ordinarily, nothing felt. But when my foot hits an uneven paving stone its resistant surface is felt in a particular way, and one which changes the organisation of space around my body so that now what was, in Heidegger's words, 'remote' is now closest to me. I may, if it is dark, say, now have to feel my way by touch. That kind of activity, like all the many examples Heidegger provides of handling tools and materials, is possible only for one whose concern with the world and whose embodiment in it are intimately linked, since it is through the body that those concerns come to light and by it that they are pursued.

'Consciousness is "I can"'

It is to Maurice Merleau-Ponty's *Phenomenology of Perception* that one turns for the development of Heidegger's comments on the body, for 'the theory of the body is', he announces, 'already a theory of perception'.[35] The starting point of Merleau-Ponty's defence of this claim is a rejection of the idea of sensation as the building blocks of our knowledge of things analogous to Heidegger's and Sartre's repudiation of it. Being able to have visual experiences conceived in terms of seeing patches of colour presupposes having experiences of things in the world, from which they are abstracted, so that, when I suddenly make out a ship with masts against the trees beyond, I only see the shapes in the light of this perception, which has a quite distinct subjective character, as we may call it, from what went before. 'Pure sensation', he says, 'is an illusion ... that causes us to put it at the beginning and to believe that it precedes knowledge ... it belongs to the domain of the constituted and not the constituting mind'.[36] Sense experience properly understood, however, is already 'inhabited with significance' in that it 'makes [the world] present as a familiar setting of our life'.[37] But this sort of significance has two aspects that Merleau-Ponty utilises his ensuing account of the body to illuminate: first, everything – the next-door house, for instance – is seen from some point of view, so that it presents just one of many possible appearances; second, everything is seen as a more-or-less determinate object against an indeterminate horizon, as Merleau-Ponty terms it, and this is to see it as a complete object and not just an appearance. 'To look at an object', he remarks, 'is to inhabit it',[38] thus metaphorically introducing a living body into the landscape it surveys.

What makes possible 'the union of the "psychic" and the "physio-logical"',[39] which the traditional picture renders mysterious, is, argues Merleau-Ponty, our being-in-the-world as a 'preobjective' relation, that is to say, one in which we are not conceived as subjects set over against objects of experience, but as embodied agents living in the world and enjoying what he terms 'operative intentionality ... which produces the natural and antepredicative unity of the world and of our life'.[40] This operative intentionality is, as for Heidegger, a matter of activity in the world. 'Consciousness is in the first place not a matter of "I think that"', as Merleau-Ponty puts it, 'but of "I can"'.[41] But Merleau-Ponty wants to explore what makes possible this bodily activity in relation to things. It requires, he says, that the body's spatiality is not a 'spatiality of position', but a 'spatiality of situation', in the sense that it is always 'directed towards a certain existing or possible task'.[42] The basic form of this is unreflected bodily movement in relation to an object in the environment, which instantiates so-called 'motor intentionality', in which the object is 'that highly specific thing towards which we project ourselves, near which we are, in anticipation, and which we haunt', rather than being 'an object represented'. It is the condition for this sort of activity that Merleau-Ponty seeks, although, as he points out, 'motor intentionality ... is concealed behind the objective world which it helps to build up'.[43]

In stressing our unreflective bodily activity in respect of things in the world Merleau-Ponty is locating something more fundamental than our relation to what Heidegger calls things ready-to-hand. For things ready-to-hand are conceptualised as tools, for example, needed for a particular task, and are recognised and utilised as such, however unmindfully. The things in our environment which we simply steer around or move aside, by contrast, need not be conceptualised in any such terms. We just have bodily capacities to deal with them that require no such higher order psychological operations. And, Merleau-Ponty maintains, even when these operations do come into play that we can deal with the things we conceptualise as we do depends upon these more basic bodily capacities – the capacities that relate us to things through what he terms 'motor intentionality'. The difference comes out in the role judgement plays in the two cases. 'Why did you pick that up?' we may ask, and be answered, 'I thought it was my coffee cup.' But if the response to 'Why did you trip?' is 'I misjudged the steps', it is not a false thought that is cited in explanation, but clumsiness, inattention, or perhaps some unfamiliar physical set-up. In any event it is, so to speak, the body that has let one down, not the mind.

This contrast can be obscured by the fact that we are normally able to specify the way we took the world to be when our bodies let us down in terms of some false belief. 'I thought the steps were shallower', we may say. But the point of this is not, in the sort of example we have in mind, to convey how we conceptualised the steps, but rather to communicate the kind of experience which led us to trip – one in which the foot goes down and does not meet the resistance of the next step at the point at which it is anticipated, in the sense of where one's foot is geared up for it to be. Grasping that kind of experience is understanding, from the agent's perspective, why he tripped. It is not just noting some physical malfunction and explaining the ensuing movement in terms of it, but seeing why, given his experience, the agent moved as he did. The point of reporting the experience in terms of a false belief is to indicate how the agent took the world to be. The automaticity of his movements does not imply that they are unconnected with the seeming glimpses of the world which his experiences provide (as one's heartbeat or breathing, say, normally are). Indeed, the motor intentionality such movements manifest is crucial to building up that world, and it is only because we, as sharing these capacities, can see that world as another agent does that we can understand why he moves as he does, now appropriately, now inappropriately to the way things are.

The notion of appropriateness at work here is not that of reasonableness, as when we explain some action in terms of the belief to which an experience gives rise: I picked something up because it looked like my coffee cup, for example, so my action was therefore reasonable in the light of my experience. That I move as I do, however, is not usually to be explained in terms of the reasonableness of such a movement, precisely because beliefs are not involved. Rather the movement may just be the right one for the configuration of surfaces about me, for their movements or for other relevant events in my environment. If it is the wrong one it is not somehow appropriate to the way I took things to be. But the way I experienced them may nevertheless explain why I failed to move appropriately. For in such circumstances I lose my usual grip on the world precisely because my body has let me down in my dealings with it. And this demonstrates the way in which one's relation to the world, taken for granted in one's usual transactions with doors, cups and so forth, depends upon the more primitive processes of motor intentionality.

What is common to Merleau-Ponty and Heidegger here, however, is that the intentionality of experience is grounded in one's concernful dealings with the world. It is these that motor intentionality serves, as much as does the intentionality involved in forming beliefs about one's environment and acting upon them as part of one's reasons for acting. Indeed, though the operations of motor intentionality do not involve the formation of beliefs, as the contrasting cases of perception do, however unreflectively, still, equipped as we are with the concepts for such beliefs, motor intentionality can provide us with reasons for them. 'I thought the steps were shallower' is what I may say, precisely because my experience gave me a reason for this belief even though the belief played no part in explaining my movement, while the experience did. The experience as of no step where it ought to be gets this content in virtue of the belief for which it provides a reason, not in virtue of any conceptual content intrinsic to it.[44] But that we can characterise the experience in this way is sufficient to establish a logical link between it and the belief for which it is a reason, albeit an uninformative link. What links the two informatively is, rather, the grasp we have of such an experience as the sort of thing that explains the movement – the extension of the leg so far and no further – a movement which would have been appropriate only if the steps had been shallower. To grasp this is to grasp how motor intentionality builds up a world within which we can pursue our purposes.

The Autonomy of the Body

Motor intentionality involves a certain kind of autonomy on the part of the body which Merleau-Ponty exemplifies through discussing a patient who is capable of what he terms 'concrete' movements but not 'abstract' ones.[45] That is to say, when asked to move specified parts of his body or report their position he is unable to do so with his eyes shut and can only do so by looking at his limbs. Yet he can move those body parts as required in ordinary actions, like blowing his nose, without any difficulty. What is clear from this is that the motor intentionality involved in his successful acts cannot involve any representation or conceptualisation of his body, since when an abstract movement requiring this is requested he cannot comply in the usual way but can otherwise perform quite normally. Rather, his body's successful dealings with objects *are* what constitutes his understanding of how it needs to move. Nor is this sort of understanding confined to parts of the body. Merleau-Ponty mentions the blind man's stick as an extension of the body in this respect, and so is the driver's car or the typist's keyboard. In each case 'it is the body which 'understands' in the cultivation of habit'.[46] And the body can act outside of what we do in what Merleau-Ponty terms our 'personal existence'. So, for example, 'while I am overcome by some grief and wholly given over to my distress, my eyes already stray in front of me, and are drawn, despite everything, to some shining object, and thereupon resume their autonomous existence.'[47] Unless the body had this sort of autonomous relation to the world we could not harness it to our personal purposes; for 'in order that we may be able to move our body towards an object, the object must first exist for it',[48] and not just be a thing represented in space.

The conditions for this are complex. They include at least the following three features which we shall discuss in turn: first, my body must not be an object for me; second, there must be a unity of the senses; and third, the body must be 'of space',[49] not merely in it. The first point recognises that in order to sense things in the world, to touch them, for example, I must not simultaneously sense my body, as touched, say. The two activities are mutually exclusive, even though, at any moment, 'when I press my two hands together ... both hands can alternate the roles of "touching" and "being touched"'.[50] The body has to be, in this sense, invisible if it is to allow us to see objects: 'bodily space [is] the background against which the object as the goal of our action may stand out of the void in front of which it may *come to light*', for the body is 'the third term, always tacitly understood in the figure-background structure'.[51] The object which is 'the goal of our action', the house I look at, say, as I point towards it, can be seen distinctly because my hand, although taking up more of my visual field, is only vaguely present to sight, since it is what orientates my body towards the house, not what my body is orientated towards (as if I were drawing it with the other hand, for instance).

It is worth noting that immediately after his principal discussion of this point – the body as in no way serving as an object when it is involved in the sensing activity necessary to motor intentionality – Merleau-Ponty briefly touches upon the way pain is experienced as localised. This does not mean, he notes, that I experience my foot, for example, as the object which causes the pain, but that I experience my foot as 'pain-infested'.[52] The body is *itself* affective, not, as Brentano, for instance, thought,[53] the object of proprioceptive sensations *accom-*

panied by aversive feelings. It is worth adding that, though the body in pain is not presented as an object, it still impedes the sensing of other objects. Sartre notices that, when my eyes start hurting as I read, still 'my body is a point of view' and not 'apprehended for itself'. But soon, 'it is with more difficulty that the words are detached from the undifferentiated ground', although this is not because my body absorbs my attention – but I can struggle on and 'forget' my pain even though it remains. 'Pain', Sartre continues, 'is totally devoid of intentionality ... it is the eyes-as-pain or vision-as-pain'.[54] A notion like that of Merleau-Ponty's motor intentionality might, perhaps, allow us to modify this statement slightly, for there are reactions to pains which identify the parts that hurt quite unreflectively – we rub the foot, screw up the eyes and so on, and such manifestations of the 'autonomous' body can get in the way of other activity.

The second condition I mentioned for motor intentionality was that the senses should operate in a unified way: the senses 'must all open on the same space'.[55] 'The unity of the senses', Merleau-Ponty maintains, 'is ... the formal expression of a fundamental contingency: the fact that we are in the world ... Every sensation is spatial ... no sensation is atomic ... all sensory experience presupposes a certain field, hence co-existence'.[56] The reason why a single spatial world is presented to the different senses is because 'the body ... tends ... towards one single goal of its activity'.[57] We are, for the most part, engaged in one activity requiring our attention: putting the kettle on, say, for a cup of tea. Now to do this I have to lift and fill it from the tap which I turn on with the other hand, all things that I can do quite automatically and which involve motor intentionality. But this requires that the handle of the kettle and the knob on the tap which I touch with my hands should be felt where I see them to be when I reach out now to the one, now the other, and that the sound of water flowing should come from the direction of the tap as located by sight and by where I feel the kettle to be as I hold it out beneath the tap. Each object is accessible to the different senses because my body relies on them together in directing its activity to each, and it is because each object in the world is so accessible that the senses constitute a unity.

That they do is what explains how it is that, though any object presents a single appearance from any one point of view, and, indeed, only a part of it is touched, it is not a single appearance or tactual image that we perceive but the object as a whole. Although I see only the front of the kettle, my hand reaches round to the handle behind and grasps it. In virtue of such facts it stands out from the vague background of objects around as a kettle, which can hold water, and which will purr into life as the water heats, producing a sound that stands out from its back-ground as I look forward to my tea. Here the movements of our own bodies are of particular significance in bringing the objects towards which they are directed into the centre of our sensory field, but our activity is triggered by events in the world as much as by our prior purposes. As we noticed in an earlier example, our eyes are drawn to some shining object, or we turn to hear a sound, and in such acts our bodies are set, as it were, to follow up by handling or looking respectively.

Not only is the unity of the senses required for motor intentionality but also for what Merleau-Ponty calls a 'body image',[58] which involves a grasp of what my body is doing although, unlike the things it is dealing with, it itself is not the object of perception. Our bodies are thus not, like such things, *in* space, but *of it* – the third condition we noted earlier. This point is closely related to Heidegger's idea that the body does not just fill up space, it 'makes room for itself', in the sense of having a capacity to assess its position in space and move itself and its parts on the basis of this capacity. Our body image involves our ability to know pre-reflectively where the parts of our body are in relation to each other and to things in our vicinity. Evidently something like this is needed for it to be able to operate successfully in relation to such things. In order to locate something by touch, for example, one must know where the hand that touches it is, though its position is known in a way different from and prior to, in one sense, the position of the table one touches. Thus,

> the thing, and the world, are given to me along with the parts of my body ... in a living connection comparable, or rather identical, with that existing between the parts of my body itself. External perception and the perception of one's own body vary in conjunction because they are two facets of one and the same act.[59]

The body image is not independent of a knowledge of the position of things so that, in another sense, this is prior: 'I know indubitably where my pipe is [when holding it], and thereby I know where my hand and my body are.'[60]

The three features we have discussed help to bring out Merleau-Ponty's conception of the way the body is required for perception of things in the world. It is so required because the motor intentionality it manifests is needed as the basis for the intentionality of objects of perception, and motor intentionality demands a body which, while itself unsensed, can sense the things its activity is directed towards, can utilise all its senses towards this single goal, and can take up positions in space appropriate to those of the things it is operating on. All these features involve a degree of autonomy on the part of the body; it gets on with things, so to speak, without being consciously controlled (though at any time it can be).

Sensitivity to Colours

Merleau-Ponty draws upon the autonomy of the body in discussing the sensory experiences involved in fully conscious perception. One way to view Merleau-Ponty's discussion is as addressing the question we noted in the first section of this chapter as exercising analytic philosophies: do sensations have so-called phenomenal or sensational content as well as having intentional objects? We saw at the outset that Merleau-Ponty rejects 'pure sensation' as an illusion and with it, we may add, the whole notion of content in terms of which the question is posed. But how, then, does he account for what it is like to have the experiences we do, particularly when we seem to be regarding them as things to savour, so that it is these that interest us rather than the things that usually engross our attention?

Merleau-Ponty is clear at the start that what we then savour is something *different* from the experience of things, not some refined component of such experience. 'The sensation of blue', he remarks, 'is not the knowledge ... of a certain identifiable *quale* throughout all the experiences of it which I have', because usually it is intentional in having a 'significance beyond itself',[61] so that depending on what thing is seen its blueness may well look different. Merleau-Ponty has a wealth of examples of things, whose colour we know, being seen in different lighting conditions which we nonetheless allow for in processing their colour. It is only when the nature of the object is obliterated, by looking at only a small part through a tube, say, that another colour is seen. When I do something analogous to this by a particular act of attention, 'when I ask myself *what precisely is it that I see* ... this attitude does away with the spectacle properly speaking', for then 'I break the link between my vision and the world'.[62] In ordinary experience, then, I just do not have a sensation in which something is larger when it is closer, for my eyes allow for such changes in my visual field and all I see is something of invariant size. Exactly the same goes for the colours of things, where lighting conditions, which may involve shadows, reflections and so forth, are similarly allowed for, since they are quite irrelevant to the object my activity is directed towards.

Yet, Merleau-Ponty maintains, there are features of sense experiences which we can access through reflecting upon what it is like to have them, but which are present in the unreflective use of them to deal with the world. His example is that of the way colours affect us differently. 'Blue is that which prompts me to look in a certain way, that which allows my gaze to run over it in a specific manner. It is a certain field or atmosphere presented to the power of my eyes and of my whole body.' It is the body here which spontaneously reacts 'in a specific manner', being drawn in, as it were, to blue and green, turned away by red and yellow, so that we are inclined to say, 'Red signifies effort or violence, green restfulness and peace.' But to understand this, Merleau-Ponty goes on, 'we must rediscover how to live these colours as our body does, that is, as peace or violence in concrete form'. For there are not *two* facts here – sensation and reaction – but rather, 'Red by its texture, as followed and adhered to by our gaze, is already the amplification of our motor being'.[63] What it is like to see something as red is, in other words, for our body to react to it in this way as a manifestation of its autonomy, to which I must give in if I am to have this kind of experience and which is a precondition of it. This relationship is expressed by Merleau-Ponty thus: 'I can see blue because I am *sensitive* to colours, whereas personal acts create a situation.' Here he denies that the traditional paradigm of subjectivity can really serve as one: 'I ought to say that *one* perceives in me, and not that I perceive',[64] for though *I* bring to perception the situation for which it is required, it is the autonomous activity of the body that makes perception possible. What this demonstrates, however, is not duality, but the necessarily embodied condition of subjectivity in which our bodily propensities towards things in the world express what it is like to experience them.

Before leaving Merleau-Ponty's discussion it is worth noticing how these ideas can be utilised in resolving a problem in analytic philosophy of how to explain various relations between colours and other visual properties which appear to be logical ones, even though these properties are, in some sense, logically simple. Towards the end of his life Wittgenstein took up again these problems which had exercised him much earlier. For example, he asks, 'Why is it that something can be transparent green but not transparent white?'[65] The answer, it has been suggested by a scientifically minded analytic philosopher, is that 'transparent white' would involve a contradiction, since to be transparent is to transmit almost all incident light, whereas to be white is to scatter almost all of it back.[66] But this cannot be the right *sort* of answer, since the high degree of reflectiveness of white surfaces cannot explain why they *look* opaque, as well as why they are; for, Wittgenstein notes, 'We don't say of something which looks transparent that it looks white.'[67]

The sort of answer suggested by Merleau-Ponty's considerations would be quite different. It might be that whiteness is the limiting case of a colour that throws the eyes back, baffling the sort of exploration that would be needed to look beneath a surface into any transparent depths beneath. White has a tendency to dazzle, and when we are dazzled, as Merleau-Ponty notes, 'no gaze is specifically directed' since 'light ... becomes painful which invades the eye itself'.[68] Less intense white is still, as Wittgenstein observes, 'cloudy',[69] so that the forms which we would need to see beneath, if a surface were transparent, are obliterated, again because our eyes cannot, as it were, penetrate the whiteness from which they are thrown back. This explanation is a phenomenological one, but one that links what an experience is like to what we are *doing* in having it, and what we are doing to the way our bodies react. And that is at a far remove from explanations in terms of physics and physiology which then leave it a mystery why the resulting experience is as it is.

Summary

Sensory perceptions and bodily sensations are paradigms of mental states that have a subjective character: there is something it is like to be in them which seems recalcitrant to explanation in terms of the way they function to mediate behaviour. Continental philosophers, like Sartre, have typically rejected accounts of this which postulate 'contents' of experience over and above the objects to which it is directed; so how is its subjective character to be explained?

Heidegger approaches the question by first asking what it is like to live in the world as we do, when it is the availability of things around us that matters, not the visual sensations and so forth which they produce. We are concerned with those, he suggests, only when things go wrong, or when we take a break from active engagement with the world. Their subjective character in these circumstances is, therefore, no indication of what experience is like for us in other situations.

Merleau-Ponty develops Heidegger's account by viewing our existence in the world as primarily 'pre-objective', that is, as that of embodied agents manipulating things unreflectively, rather than that of subjects set over against the objects of our experience. Intentionality is in the first place, therefore, the 'motor intentionality' of my body acting, as it were, autonomously upon objects. It is motor intentionality which gives us, literally as well as metaphorically, a grasp on objects, so that they are perceived as complete things, even though they project only a two-dimensional image on our retinas. Here, as elsewhere, Merleau-Ponty explains what an experience is like in terms of our bodily propensities to act in relation to it.

For neither philosopher, however, is what our experience is like exhausted by an account of its intentional content. This content captures what the experience gives us grounds, other things being equal, for believing about the world, whether such a belief is reflective or merely presupposed by the way we unreflectively act. But we can allow that experiences can ground the same belief and yet differ in their subjective character without postulating some mysterious phenomenal content. Rather they differ in ways that reflect our different modes of engagement with the world and the distinctive ways in which our bodies react to things in these modes. Typically such experiences will differ in the attitudes or feelings towards things that they involve, as in the difference between casually taking in familiar surroundings and cautiously observing unfamiliar ones, or between merely being aware of the colours of things and becoming absorbed in them. We grasp what such experiences are like because we have shared bodily reactions, for reasons both physiological and cultural, and we can therefore see how, in certain circumstances, someone can have a reason for reacting as they do, as well as for the beliefs about the world she is thereby led to form.

Notes

1. Thomas Nagel, *Mortal Questions* (Cambridge: Cambridge University Press, 1979), ch. 12.
2. E.g. John McDowell, *Mind and World* (Cambridge, MA: Harvard University Press, 1994).
3. See Marie McGinn, *Wittgenstein and the 'Philosophical Investigations'* (London: Routledge, 1997), chs 4–5.
4. Which may not actually exist.
5. Franz Brentano, *Psychology from an Empirical Standpoint* (London: Routledge & Kegan Paul, 1973).
6. Jean-Paul Sartre, *Being and Nothingness* (London: Methuen, 1969), p. xxxvi.
7. Ibid., p. xxii.
8. Ibid., p. xl.
9. Jean-Paul Sartre, *The Transcendence of the Ego* (New York: Hill & Wang, 1990), p. 31.
10. Sartre, *Being and Nothingness*, pp. xxx, xxxii.
11. Ibid., p. 308.
12. Ibid., pp. xxi, xxxviii.
13. Martin Heidegger, *Being and Time* (Oxford: Blackwell, 1969), H 143 (references are to the original German as is the convention).
14. Ibid., H 42.
15. Ibid., H 46.
16. Ibid., H 61.
17. Ibid., H 163–4.
18. Ibid., H 69.

19. Quoted J. P. Fell, 'The Familiar and the Strange: On the Limits of Practice in the Early Heidegger', in Hubert L. Dreyfus and Harrison Hall (eds), *Heidegger: A Critical Reader* (Oxford: Blackwell, 1992), p. 66.
20. Heidegger, *Being and Time*, H 67.
21. Ibid., H 42.
22. Ibid., H 73.
23. Ibid., H 57.
24. Ibid., H 172.
25. Ibid., H 146.
26. Ibid., H 147.
27. Ibid., H 135.
28. Ibid., H 108.
29. E.g. ibid., H 48, 56, 368.
30. Ibid., H 368.
31. Ibid., H 106.
32. Ibid., H 107.
33. Ibid., H 97.
34. Ibid., H 137.
35. Maurice Merleau-Ponty, *Phenomenology of Perception* (London: Routledge & Kegan Paul, 1962), p. 203.
36. Ibid., p. 37.
37. Ibid., pp. 52–3.
38. Ibid., p. 80.
39. Ibid., p. 80.
40. Ibid., p. xviii.
41. Ibid., p. 137.
42. Ibid., p. 100.
43. Ibid., p. 138 n. 2.
44. *Pace* McDowell, *Mind and World*, who thinks that experiences cannot provide reasons without such conceptual content.
45. Merleau-Ponty, *Phenomenology*, pp. 103–13.
46. Ibid., p. 144.
47. Ibid., p. 84.
48. Ibid., p. 139.
49. Ibid., p. 148.
50. Ibid., p. 93.
51. Ibid., pp. 101–2.
52. Ibid., p. 93.
53. Brentano, *Psychology*, pp. 82–3, 145.
54. Sartre, *Being and Nothingness*, pp. 331–2.
55. Merleau-Ponty, *Phenomenology*, p. 217.
56. Ibid., p. 56.
57. Ibid., p. 232.
58. Ibid., pp. 98–147.
59. Ibid., p. 205.
60. Ibid., p. 100.
61. Ibid., p. 123.
62. Ibid., pp. 226–7.
63. Ibid., pp. 210–11.

64. Ibid., p. 215.
65. Ludwig Wittgenstein, *Remarks on Colour* (Oxford: Blackwell, 1977), I 19.
66. J. Westphal, 'White', *Mind*,1986, pp. 311–28.
67. Wittgenstein, *Remarks on Colour*, III 153.
68. Merleau-Ponty, *Phenomenology*, p. 315.
69. Wittgenstein, *Remarks on Colour*, III 4–5, 7.

2

The Constraints of Experience

Experience and Externality

Let us suppose that we reject the 'myth of the given' or the idea of 'contents' of consciousness whose character explains what it is like to have our experiences, and adopt instead an account in terms of the ways things can become intentional objects of experience through the manner of our bodily interactions with them. This may still leave us with the uneasy feeling that something the 'given' was meant to suggest has dropped out of our story, namely, the way in which our perceptions and especially our bodily sensations are not only what we *make* of them – not only, indeed, how our bodily reactions give shape to them. For our bodily reactions are reactions to what we experience, which is seemingly not exhausted by the intentional objects constituted in the course of our purposeful activity in the world. And this seems to leave out the brute – indeed, sometimes brutal – irruption of many of our sensations into such activity, so that it is not their relevance to it, but their utter independence of it, and thus of the world in which it takes place, that characterises their impact as, so to speak, 'given'.

What is required is an account of how our experiences reveal something beyond the subject qua agent; for even in the case of bodily sensations like pain there is something – our bodies – that experience directs our attention to. The required account cannot be provided simply in terms of the intentional objects of experience, however, if their intentionality is cashed out, as we so far see it to be, through the ways in which an agent relates to the world of her activity. Even if the *bodily* character of this activity is emphasised, and even if the autonomy of the body relative to the agent's reflective purposes is stressed, it is still the body as active, as what embodies agency, that is involved, and not the body as passive, as something acted upon from outside.

There is, then, a problem here which confronts accounts of experience which, like Heidegger's and Merleau-Ponty's, follow the Kantian approach in locating what is given in experience in terms of some features of the experiencing subject. For, instead of Kant's forms of intuition – space and time – under which we must bring objects, Heidegger and Merleau-Ponty substitute our practical concerns with the world, through whose salience to which things are constituted as the intentional objects of perception. The problem is that it becomes unclear how our experiences can exert the required control, from outside, as it were, upon our thoughts and actions. True, we are receptive in respect of them – only their form, so to say, depends on us – but it is still mysterious what our experiences must be like in order to reveal to us the way things are. We want somehow to grasp this from within, without, *per impossibile*, going beyond our forms of intuition or their equivalent, to a reality beyond. We do not want simply to be told that we are so set up as to respond with the appropriate belief given the corresponding stimulus.

It is useful here to compare some of the authors we shall consider with the account of experience offered by John McDowell,[1] which is itself a broadly Kantian one. McDowell is concerned to defend what he terms a 'minimal empiricism' according to which beliefs are directed towards the world through being answerable to experience. But, he continues, in order to provide the reasons for beliefs which such answerability requires, experience must be logically linked to beliefs, and this in turn, he argues, implies that it must already be conceptualised. Thus our experiences involve spontaneity in their conceptualisation, but also receptivity, which enables them to act as a constraint upon the beliefs they ground. To suppose that what is conceptualised is some 'extra-conceptual deliverance of receptivity' is to fall back into the myth of the given, and to break the logical link between experience and belief. As McDowell puts it, 'in experience one finds oneself saddled with content',[2] and this passivity is what acts as an empirical constraint, not something acting upon one from outside, as it were, of one's way of conceiving the world.

Now the mystery mentioned a moment ago attends McDowell's account. For, from within, all we are permitted to notice is that we are 'saddled' with having to conceptualise our environment in a particular way. This is not, McDowell wants to insist, simply the inexplicable onset of an inclination to judge that things are thus and so. In such a picture, he rightly observes, 'the experience itself goes missing'.[3] But all McDowell offers us instead is the assurance that our inclination to judge is not inexplicable because we have a reason for judging – and that is true. Yet he does nothing to show how we can understand experience as providing us with such a reason. The experience itself consists simply in the application of concepts which we apprehend as providing us with reasons for belief, reasons which can be overridden in cases like the Muller-Lyer illusion, for example. And the complaint is not, of course, that there are non-representational properties of the experience in virtue of which such concepts are applied. It is that we only understand what it is to apply those concepts because the experience gives us a prima facie reason for judging them to apply, and it does this in virtue, not of intrinsic properties, but of its wider place in our lives, on which McDowell is largely silent.

The implausibility of McDowell's account appears most vividly in his treatment of the deliverances of 'inner sense' – our experiences of bodily sensations and the like. For them too, McDowell insists, 'we need to conceive them, like the impressions of 'outer sense' as themselves possessing conceptual content ... passive occurrences in which conceptual capacities are drawn into operation'.[4] But, unlike outer sense, inner sense does not make us aware of circumstances obtaining independently of our experiences of them, so that the judgments we form on the basis of them are about the impressions themselves, not about something else which they are impressions of. So insistent is he that our experience of pain and so forth has conceptual content that McDowell castigates Wittgenstein for likening avowals of pain to expressions of pain such as moaning, which may seem to deny them genuine judgmental status. Yet Wittgenstein's point is surely that we can understand them as judgments for which our experience provides a reason only because we can *moan* them out. Without that linkage they would be inexplicable and we would fail to grasp the character of an experience on which they were supposedly based.

What we shall be doing in what follows is to explain how continental thinkers have tried to expose the linkage between experience and life in virtue of which our thoughts are intelligibly constrained by what experience reveals to us. Each tries, in a different way, to escape the problem for accounts inspired by Kant – the problem of seeing our experience as something more than simply what we make of it through constituting its intentional objects, without falling back into a myth of the given that turns it into the apprehension of bare presences. Heidegger himself, in his later work, had wished to make this so-called 'turn', viewing 'man in his essence [as] eksistent into the openness of Being, into the open region that lights the "between" within which a "relation" of subject to object can "be"'.[5] The subject/object relation in terms of which Being is thought of as revealed to Dasein in *Being and Time* is here seen as derivative from a situation in which one is 'open' to the way things are, prior to intentional engagement with them. But

Heidegger does not take us far towards a grasp of this situation, for which we must look elsewhere.

The Flesh

We can start by looking at how Merleau-Ponty develops his own account in order to address the problem of capturing the given character of experience. 'The vision we acquire seems to come to us', from the things we see, so that 'my look enveloping them does not hide them'.[6] That, then, is the problem. How does the contribution I make to seeing something through the way I look at it nonetheless result in my seeing it as it is, because it controls my seeing? How, Merleau-Ponty asks, does 'my look ... veiling [things], unveil them?'

In answering this question Merleau-Ponty draws upon two features of his earlier account, but he develops it in a new direction. First he reminds us that perceiving things is a process in which the senses are active. 'The look ... envelops, palpates ... visible things.' That is to say, it actively examines them, but in doing so 'it moves in its own way with its abrupt and imperious style'.[7] Similarly I feel textures only through movements of my hands against them, but, again, largely involuntary movements. What is happening here brings in the second feature of his earlier account, the 'anonymity' or autonomy of the body, its moving of its own accord. But here Merleau-Ponty interprets these movements through which things are perceived as somehow suited to those things, such that 'finally one cannot say if it is the look or if it is the things that command'.[8] The movements of the eyes required to see something are responsive to the sort of thing it is, while it could only appear as it is given these movements. What controls the senses is here presented, however, as the things they sense. The autonomy of their operation is not, as seems to be implied in the earlier work of Merleau-Ponty, to be explained in terms of the way it serves our active engagement with a world we constitute in the light of its relevance to our purposes. Rather, although the operation of the senses does indeed do that, it is something more primitive than this engagement. It is what is required for that engagement to be controlled by confrontation with the deliverances of experience, rather than simply by the *mysterious* fulfilment or frustration of our purposes. How is it, though, that sensory experience can reveal something beyond itself?

Merleau-Ponty's answer is that it can do so only because seen and seer are, as he puts it, introducing a new metaphorical term into his discussion, of the same *flesh*. The word has connotations of carnality and sensuality, but also of the incarnation of what is, in some sense, transcendent. The notion, Merleau-Ponty concedes, 'has no name in any philosophy', and as such is hard to expound, for it signifies 'the formative medium of the object or the subject'[9] and thus 'not ... matter, not mind ... not substance' not 'the union or compound of two substances', but rather an '"element" in the sense of a *general* thing, midway between the spatio-temporal individual and the idea'. What the notion is meant to explain is, as he carries on, the fact that, for example, 'the hidden face of the cube radiates forth somewhere as well as does the face I have under my eyes',[10] which is not merely to say that, as we noticed in the preceding chapter, we see whole objects rather than their frontal appearances, but that these objects are seen as similarly visible from elsewhere, just as we ourselves are, that visibility is a feature of things. This presupposes, Merleau-Ponty maintains, something beyond individual seers which makes their seeing possible.

Merleau-Ponty's argument to this conclusion, to the existence of what he terms the flesh, turns crucially on the notion of *reversibility*. What shows that the seer and the seen exist in the same element is that the seer can herself be seen, that there is a 'coiling over of the visible upon the seeing body', such that 'my body sees only because it is part of the visible in which it opens forth'. In particular, Merleau-Ponty suggests, 'as soon as we see other seers ... we are for ourselves fully visible ... For the first time the seeing that I am is really visible',[11] though he is here dramatising something that is taken for granted in our experience, rather than indicating a special formative experience. Jacques Lacan – one of many French philosophers influenced by Merleau-Ponty's account later – illustrated the point that 'we are beings who are looked at, in the spectacle of the world. That which makes us consciousness institutes us by the same token as *speculum mundi*.'[12] A shining object, such as, he suggests, a sunlit sardine can floating in the sea, can catch my eye, indicating a point from which I could be seen – a realisation implicit in my looking at it. This is something more, though, than simply my location as a seer in a public space of visible things. For my visibility implies that I am more than just a seer; I am a bodily thing, the movements of whose sense organs required for sensing are movements of that body which are themselves potentially available to the senses.

Merleau-Ponty's key example of reversibility is, however, touch. With touch, we can touch *ourselves* in a way not possible for vision, namely, touch the hand that touches, so that the existence of each in the same element is assured. 'Since the same body sees and touches,' Merleau-Ponty continues, 'visible and tangible belong to the same world.'[13] Where he goes beyond *Phenomenology of Perception* here is in deriving the conclusion that not only are common objects of sight and touch constituted by a motor intentionality which harnesses both senses in a single activity but that, prior to that intentionality, there is a certain sort of body. It is, he says, 'the thickness of the body' that is 'the sole means I have to go unto the heart of the things, by making myself a world and by making them flesh'.[14]

In touching myself, the hand that touches is itself touched, and this ensures that the touching is part of the world that is touched. It is not something that has, qua experiencing, an existence outside that world; nor is what is experienced, the touched hand, something that could possibly be simply a thing constituted by the touching, since it is itself something that touches. While Merleau-Ponty concedes that the human body is 'a very remarkable variant'[15] on things in the world, since it can be both subject and object, it is of the same 'flesh' as them, and as such is neither essentially subject nor object. Indeed, Merleau-Ponty thinks that, in my touching myself, the subject/object relation cannot be discerned because of its reversibility.

Merleau-Ponty's argument is that experience reveals something beyond itself only because it is the experience of creatures themselves situated among such things as equally the objects of possible experiences. It is what the experiencer and the experienced have in common – the 'flesh' – that allows the former to apprehend the latter as other than itself. But this common element is prior to, though presupposed in, any world-making activity in which subjects engage. It is the 'formative medium' of both subject and object brought into relation by such world-making, because the subject would not be a being *in* the world of her activity unless she shared something with its objects. But this must, therefore, be something prior to their constitution as objects. It is that she is something over and above a subject in the world of her making which is responsible for their having an existence over and above being objects in that world. And what she has is a *fleshly* existence which the passivity of outer experiences – be they experiences of being touched or, indeed, of having one's eye caught by something – reveals, just as much as inner ones such as pain do. It is an existence as something other than a subject, an otherness within the very body without which she could not be a subject.

The notion of the 'flesh' may well seem rebarbative to Anglo-Saxon philosophers, influential though it has been on the Continent. While it would be presumptuous to recast it in more congenial terms, there are, it may be suggested, aspects of the notion that indicate how one might account for the way the deliverances of experience can constrain our thoughts about the world. It is because our bodies are like the things we touch and see that our experiences can deliver information about such things, for, in being touched and seen, they have an effect upon our bodies which is possible only in virtue of this commonality and which is necessary for them to be experienced. Merleau-Ponty's model for this is the way I feel the sensation of being touched as I press my own hand against myself. But this is not simply a causal connection whereby the experience is the effect of something impinging upon my sense organs. For the effect is itself felt: I feel myself being touched or the shining sardine can catching my eye.

These felt effects do provide a reason for my responsive movements – recoiling from a cold touch, say, or involuntarily glancing towards a point of light – even prior to any conceptualisation. They do so in virtue of the fact that we all respond in the same way to such things; our bodies possess what Merleau-Ponty terms a 'concordant operation' which renders our experiences unmysterious to each other, and in this way a reason for our actions. It is this similarity of operation in our bodies, independent of individual will and present purpose, which leads Merleau-Ponty to speak of the senses as anonymous: 'it is not I who sees, not he who sees, because an anonymous visibility inhabits both of us, a vision in general, in virtue of that primordial property that belongs to the flesh ... of radiating everywhere and forever'.[16] It is this primitive intersubjectivity which allows our thoughts to be about, and to be constrained by, a common empirical world. The constraints are grounded in causal mechanisms, but what makes them rational constraints is the commonality of those mechanisms which is necessary for, but prior to, conceptualisation.

In response to such a picture, however, McDowell[17] could reply that we have provided an exteriority only by returning to a picture of givenness linked only causally to potential judgements or bodily reactions, reactions we might share, for example, simply in virtue of having the same kind of biological bodies. Haven't we lost what he had been so anxious to highlight, namely, the content of experience as justifying, providing reasons for, the judgments we might make on the basis of it? It is this demand which had led McDowell to insist that the contents of experience must be conceptualised. In dissenting from McDowell's account of reason, which requires conceptualisations which can feature in sequences of reflective reasoning, we nonetheless recognise that our experiences justify, make appropriate, our responses, judgemental or otherwise, to them. The causal picture outlined above might be that of a detached observer. It does not capture the perspective of subjects within the world whose experiences the authors we have been discussing are at pains to delineate. To those subjects their responses are intelligible in a rationalising rather than causal way. What grounds the intelligibility here is an implicit publicness. We are in the world among others who respond in parallel ways, or can be brought to do so when exposed to shared elements of experience. This does not mean that all our responses, even to bodily sensations, are the same. Differences of response may mark differently abled bodies, or a different complexity of situation. The responses are, however, publicly recognisable. From them we grasp elements of the experience, not inductively, as hypothesised causes, but as that which renders them intelligible and appropriate.

The Indeterminacy of Experience

Jean-François Lyotard also pursues the question of accounting for the fact, as he puts it, that there is some event; and he does this in the context of trying to escape the structuralist idea that all there is is discourse, or, in Merleau-Ponty's terms, all we grasp in perception is what we have contributed to it through the intentional objects we have constituted. He describes his influential book, *Discourse, Figure*, as 'a defence of the eye, its localisation. It has darkness as its prey. The twilight which after Plato's word threw a grey veil over sensibility ... this twilight is the interest of this book.'[18] This last point hints at his criticism of Merleau-Ponty. Commenting on his notion of the flesh, Lyotard notes that 'Merleau-Ponty wants to move from the I to the One' (i.e. to the impersonal medium of the flesh). But, he continues, a 'pre-conceptual system ... like every system' is not able to account for 'the fact that there are events (in the visual field or elsewhere), but precisely for the fact that the event ... is absorbed ... into a world'. That there *are* events cannot be explained, because Merleau-Ponty's is 'still a reflection on *knowledge*, and the function of such a reflection is to absorb the event, to recuperate the Other into the Same'.[19]

Lyotard's criticism here parallels those made by Emmanuel Levinas, whom we shall discuss in the next section. Merleau-Ponty has shown, writes Levinas, 'the I that constitutes the world comes up against a sphere in which it is by its very flesh implicated ... in what it otherwise would have constituted and so is implicated in the world'.[20] But Levinas does not believe this fact about the self – the 'Same' as he, prior to Lyotard, terms it – can establish anything beyond it – anything about the 'Other'. For Levinas too regards Merleau-Ponty as concerned with a relationship of knowledge between self and world, when what is needed is an account of how there can be anything to be known. These criticisms are, perhaps, unfair on Merleau-Ponty, who regards his notion of the flesh as pointing to a precondition for knowledge, a precondition that does indeed take the subject beyond herself to some 'event'. The subject's

fleshly involvement in the world is not itself a primitive kind of knowledge, unlike, it would seem, Merleau-Ponty's earlier 'motor intentionality'. Yet it is true that the 'event' of which we become aware through
experience remains – perhaps deliberately, since it is not yet an
intentional object – mysterious in Merleau-Ponty's account, and it is
this mystery Lyotard seeks to dispel.

How can the existence of the 'event' be explained? Lyotard's answer
is complex, but it turns on the distinction between the grasp of an object
which involves looking at it, focusing, identifying, making it the centre
of attention – the activities with which Merleau-Ponty is most concerned
– and 'the first peripheral contact with something' such that 'any
attempt to *grasp* it loses it'. It is 'this fragile oblique tact' which 'gives
the visual event'.[21] Insofar as what it is like to experience this can be
presented, it is done, Lyotard suggests, through paintings like those of
Cezanne (about whom Merleau-Ponty had also written) who sits with
immobile eyes before Mont Sainte-Victoire. Such paintings offer what
Lyotard calls 'figures', as opposed to symbols, so that they are not, as
on a structuralist account, to be read. Rather their subversive rhythms
are to be responded to in a dance-like way. This mirrors the diffuse
activity of the eyes prior to focusing upon some particular object, whose
status as participant in an 'event' derives from its prior existence in this
indeterminate, unstable zone of experience. It is perhaps, worth noticing that, despite Lyotard's strictures on phenomenology, he is here
relying on methods like Merleau-Ponty's earlier ones, but whereas the
latter is concerned with what an experience is like when the eyes fasten
upon a thing, the former treats of what it is like when they do not, but
still in terms of the eye's response.

It is clear that Lyotard is less interested here in the way that what is
experienced exerts some specific control upon our thought and more in
what it is about experience that allows it to be about anything at all. He
links the notion of the 'figures' which I apprehend with the idea of
reference, which cannot be captured simply in terms of what concepts I
apply, but only by their application to something. Before I focus on
something and make it the intentional object of my visual experience, I
must be looking in the right direction, and its prior existence in this as
yet undifferentiated space is what allows me to focus on it, to point to
it, to refer. Without this categorial difference between diffuse and focal
vision there could not be, Lyotard implies, the referring of an intentional object to some 'event' in which the world impinges upon me.
Thus, while Merleau-Ponty illustrates such an impingement with cases
like something catching my eye, Lyotard finds in experience a space
from within which my eye is caught, and he views this as necessary for it

to become an experience of something catching it from outside. One might add that, by contrast, the after-image of the sun, say, cannot be focused upon and brought out of its vague surroundings into distinct visibility. In this regard its effect, so to speak, upon us is quite different from that of the bright object and, for this reason, unlike that object it cannot be referred to something beyond our experience.

A key feature of diffuse vision is its indeterminacy; and even when I focus upon something there is still – and necessarily – an area of indeterminacy round about it. My eye can move around a figure, prior to recognising it, making sense of it, conceptualising it, only because its ground is unexplored, indistinct. The indeterminacy of sensory experience is crucial to its being experience at all, rather than, say, mental imagery, which is, typically, open to invention rather than exploration, so that its lacunae are to be filled, not focused upon. An account of experience which, like McDowell's, omits this feature of experience in favour of total conceptualisation does not do justice to the phenomena. For what the indeterminacy of an experience makes room for is the way it can ground a range of judgments about the world. Of course if we were to describe the experiences that led us to say both that there was something red and that there was something round we would report them as experiences of redness and of roundness, and focusing on the colour *is* different from focusing on the shape. But it would, in most circumstances, be unrealistic to distinguish two experiences here, rather than one which could yield a variety of determinations. Indeed, the unity of experience, the way that colours and shapes can be unified into a single experience, is one of the things that distinguishes experience from thought; and this unity depends upon indeterminacy, for it is because of its indeterminacy that a single experience can ground an indefinite number of judgments, whose experiential grounds are thus unified.

It is a consequence of the indeterminacy of experience that it is always in excess of any particular way of characterising it in terms of its intentional objects. This is not to say that it has some non-representational content of the sort we investigated and dismissed in the previous chapter. For such non-representational content would still be determinate, only featuring in a supposedly different space from that of a system of concepts. It is rather to say that experience exceeds any particular characterisation in potentially grounding other judgments than those which that characterisation grounds. This is, for Lyotard, the reason why experience can be something other than just what we project upon the world, and hence why it can vouchsafe an 'event' in the world as what it gives access to. For experience exceeds any projection we make in characterising the world of our experience in terms of its intentional objects. And it does this because of its residual indeterminacy, which, Lyotard observes, is given phenomenologically.

It may seem that we are here being invited to accept Lyotard's argument simply by entertaining certain sorts of images of experience, and, in using examples from art, he does not entirely escape this danger, which could lead us back to looking for the non-representational properties rejected in the last chapter. But, at his best, Lyotard does connect the features of experience he wishes to stress to our bodily reactions, the different ways our eyes move and so on. Over and above this he links the figural, non-conceptionalised aspect of experience to desire. 'The figural', he remarks, 'is hand in glove with desire.'[22] For what it is that is desirable about something is typically just what cannot be conceptualised in the ordinary way.

Here we may recall Kant's claim that 'the judgment of taste does depend upon a concept ... but one from which nothing can be cognised in respect of the object ... because it is itself indeterminable and useless for knowledge'. An aesthetic concept applies, Kant claims, simply because 'it acquires ... validity for everyone ... because its determining ground lies, perhaps, in the concept of what may be regarded as the supersensible substrate of humanity'.[23] To the extent to which we understand why another desires something on the basis of her experience, we do so only because we might have this reaction ourselves – we share her tastes. But, unlike shared cognitive judgments, these reactions are not based on concepts systematically applicable whatever our desires. Such concepts could apply equally to two objects which yet elicit distinct reactions in respect of our desires. That the same experience can be a reason for desire as well as for belief is, however, essential to experience, and this provides Lyotard with further grounds for holding that it cannot be exhausted by concepts. It may also be why he objects to Merleau-Ponty's account as limited to the relationship of knowledge, since desire is no such cognitive relation and yet essentially a relation, if satisfied, to something beyond its subject, a relation expressed in physical action upon that object.

Pain and Enjoyment

As already indicated, Lyotard's work owes some of its ideas to Emmanuel Levinas. Levinas was a contemporary of Sartre and Merleau-Ponty and was, like them, heavily influenced by Heidegger, but who critically develops Heidegger's thinking in a different way. In particular, like the other authors we are looking at in this chapter, Levinas is concerned to see how, in experience, we can encounter something beyond ourselves; since if the significance of experience is exhausted by that which we give it, then, it would seem, we can learn nothing from it. And yet we do, for experience controls our thinking; and it does so only because it sets up a relationship with alterity, with what is other than ourselves. Like Lyotard later, Levinas looks for particular sorts of experience as revealing this otherness.

In an early work, Levinas identifies the experience of something else existing not in perception at all, but in 'the monotonous presence that bears down on us in insomnia', that is to say, in the night where precisely nothing can be perceived and which is, for just this reason, horrific: 'this void of sensations constitutes a mute, absolutely indeterminate menace'.[24] It is in an experience like this that alterity is revealed, Levinas argues, precisely because there is *nothing* that we actively bring to it. 'To be conscious is to be torn away from the *there is*',[25] he writes, and he has in mind here being conscious of some object in perception. Even if we imagine this object not existing, he suggests in a Cartesian vein, 'the fact of existing imposes itself where there is no longer anything. And it is anonymous: there is neither anyone nor anything that takes this existence upon itself. It is impersonal.'[26] Something beyond the subject of experience, the mere fact of something else existing, is encountered paradigmatically in the passivity of experiences *not* directed at any object.

Passivity is a key theme in Levinas's account, and there are elements of it which are echoed in Lyotard's notion of the indeterminate, though, as we shall see, Levinas proceeds rather differently. For Levinas wishes to distinguish the passive aspect of sensation, which may yield enjoyment or suffering, 'whose status is not reducible to being put before a spectator subject',[27] from the active aspect, which does bring about the appearance of things in the subject's world. To some extent this mirrors Lyotard's distinction between the perception of figures which induces desire and that of conceptualised objects which grounds knowledge. But Levinas is wary of a notion of 'immediate consciousness merely as a still confused representation to be duly brought to "light"', in which 'the obscure context of whatever is thematised is converted by reflection, or intentional consciousness, into clear and distinct data, like those which present the perceived world'.[28] Rather he looks for forms of consciousness which are not only, as the quotation above suggests, 'pre-reflective', but also betoken an aspect of our lives more fundamental than the active engagement presupposed in perceiving a world of objects.

The paradigm of sensations in which the passive aspect is overwhelmingly dominant is pain rather than visual perception. 'The passivity of suffering is more profoundly passive', writes Levinas, 'than the receptivity of our senses, which is already the activity of welcome and straight away becomes perception.'[29] Pain is 'profoundly passive', he continues, because it is more than just a limitation on our freedom, something which interferes with our activity; it is something to which we can attribute neither a use nor a meaning. It is worth considering the significance of these two points.

Levinas considers an objection to the suggestion that pain is useless. Might one not discover in it 'the role of an alarm signal manifesting itself for the preservation of life against the cunning dangers which menace life in illness?' He answers it only by mocking 'the grand idea necessary to the inner peace of souls in our distressed world'.[30] But perhaps one should take more seriously the common idea of pain as a form of perception of a bodily ill. Levinas provides some of the materials for this. He compares what he refers to as the 'psychological content' of suffering and of 'the lived experience of colour, of sound, of contact' but, unlike these, suffering's 'content' cannot be assembled into 'order and meaning', not because of its 'excessive intensity', but because 'suffering is at once what disturbs order and this disturbance itself'.[31] What I am conscious of in pain is not something which I could 'synthesise' into knowledge, and Levinas refers to Kant here. Indeed, his point recalls one of Kant's distinctions:

> That subjective side of a representation *which is incapable of becoming an element of cognition* is the *pleasure or displeasure* connected with it: for through it I cognise nothing in the object of the representation, although it may easily be the result of the operation of some cognition or other.[32]

In the case of pain there is no such 'cognition', and the 'subjective side' totally dominates the sensation as what makes any cognition – of bodily harm, for example – impossible, because it disturbs the activity required for cognition.

Perhaps to illustrate this Levinas might have used the following sort of example: I run my hand over a surface, feeling its warmth, and suddenly I am burned by a particularly hot area. There is a discontinuity here which does not amount to an intensified or self-directed reaction, as when the surface feels a lot hotter, or when from feeling a rough surface I now feel my skin rubbed. It is my hand that hurts, certainly, and my hand that I may involuntarily shake in the air to cool it. Yet my attention in the sudden pain was turned neither to the surface nor to my hand, neither to the world nor to my body, but to the pain. 'Suffering is experienced as being closed up in the self par excellence; this superiorly passive passion is like an impossibility of "getting out of oneself"',[33] writes Levinas, capturing the way pain absorbs the patient to the exclusion of any acts of intentionality. Thus 'pain ... remains undiluted and isolates itself in consciousness, or absorbs the rest of consciousness'.[34] And, if some form of motor intentionality is suggested as that which makes the hand that hurts an object, it might be replied that, while we do indeed rub parts that ache, just as we scratch those that itch, often without noticing the sensations responded to, this does nothing to account for the *suffering* of pain, and hence why it would, on the account being discussed, be an *ill*, an evil that was responded to.

Suffering, Levinas says, is not only 'what disturbs order' it is 'this disturbance itself', and this explains his claim that its passivity is not just 'a blow against ... freedom', but an 'evil which rends the humanity of the suffering person, overwhelms his humanity otherwise than non-freedom overwhelms it: violently and cruelly, more irremissibly than the negation which dominates or paralyzes the act in non-freedom'.[35] We may recall here Sartre's account of pain in the eye, which impedes reading. What constitutes the suffering of pain, Levinas argues, is not that it disturbs such activity. Nor, we might add, could it be claimed that it has a meaning which derives from the fact that it does so. The 'disturbance' that is suffering is independent of and prior to any activity in which I might be engaged, including, as we have seen, the activity involved in any kind of cognition. For this reason it lacks a place in the subject's world, yet, like the horror of insomnia, points towards something beyond the subject, from which, so to speak, it comes.

Yet it is not only in suffering and insomnia that Levinas locates an experience of something other, of alterity, but also in what he takes to be our basic relation to things, *jouissance* – enjoyment. It is here that he departs most fundamentally from Heidegger. 'Doing, labour, already implies the relation with the transcendent', but this is a relation to 'objects of enjoyment', not to 'objects of representation'. One 'lives *from*' such objects, as Levinas puts it, for example, from the bread one eats which is not somehow a tool or 'means of life' but, rather, that which satisfies a need. But this need is not given as the prior absence of something, subsequently recognised as satisfying it. It is identified as need because suffering, is 'a failing of happiness', in which we are cruelly denied objects of enjoyment, and this brings into focus the alterity of those objects themselves as necessary to our lives.[36] Prior to what Levinas terms 'labour' – the engaged activity with the world of represented things which Heidegger takes as fundamental – there are, then, experiences of enjoyment or suffering, without which such activity would have no point. So the incidents of rest and disinterested absorption in the world of the senses, which Heidegger treats as secondary, are primary in Levinas's account.

How does this story throw light on the nature of experience? It does so because Levinas links enjoyment with the operation of sensibility, 'which is the *mode* of enjoyment'. 'One does not know,' claims Levinas, 'one lives sensible qualities; the green of these leaves, the red of this sunset.' This relation is prior to that with objects, for though 'the sensible objects we enjoy' – bread, for example – 'have already undergone labour ... contentment in its naivete, lurks behind the relation with things'.[37] This is not, however, a return to the myth of the given, since Levinas further connects sensibility with primitive bodily reactions. He comments,

> This is the profound insight Descartes had when he refused sense data the status of clear and distinct ideas, ascribed them to the body, and relegated them to the useful. This is his superiority over Husserlian phenomenology which puts no limit on noematization.[38]

That is, to making things intentional objects of experience and as such 'clear' because comprehensible within a system of representation. Instead, argues Levinas, there are primitive physical reactions exemplified in our various kinds of enjoyment of things – or in our dislike of them – which stand behind the active physical engagement which constitutes them as objects. And these primitive reactions reflect 'the body indigent and naked',[39] as the source of need and seat of enjoyment in its satisfaction. The cry of pain, as much as joy, is an example of such a primitive reaction, in a line of thought reminiscent of the later Wittgenstein's account, which we mentioned earlier.

Where Levinas goes beyond Wittgenstein, however, is in associating the physicality of sensations with their manifestation of something beyond our consciousness of objects, which allows those objects to be not merely what we constitute in conceptualising them. His argument turns on the coincidence between the lived body and the physical body – 'this body, a sector of an elemental reality, is also what permits taking hold of the world, labouring'. But this body is that which is 'in the *other*', when it enjoys the sensations which it receives, making us, as Levinas expresses it, 'at home' in our world, so that 'the dwelling which lodges and prolongs life, the world life acquires and utilises by labour, is also the physical world'.[40] In this state of enjoyment of experienced things the distinction between passivity and activity disappears, only to be reasserted when we are not at home among them but encounter things as strange, so that we are menaced by the insecurity exemplified by pain or by insomnia. In that situation, one may say, the cry is wrung from us, is a reaction of our bodies with which we can no longer identify.

Like Lyotard after him, Levinas is less interested in the specific control that a particular experience exerts upon our thoughts about the world than in the way experience opens us up to something other than ourselves. Even more radically than Merleau-Ponty or Lyotard he denies that this is captured by reflection upon knowledge or even upon what is a precondition for knowledge. Indeed it is not the way experience controls our thoughts that is, he thinks, fundamental, but the way it controls reactions that express states of enjoyment or suffering, which are more basic than intentional thoughts. It is the very experiences of so-called 'inner sense' which present a problem for McDowell that are, paradoxically, the ones that open us up, in the first instance, to something other, for there is nothing in what *we* contribute to them – by way of conceptualisation, for example – that can explain the reactions they elicit.[41]

The moral to be drawn is that any kind of analysis which abstracts from the role of the experience in life is too like the discredited model of seeking out the phenomenal or sensational properties of an experience, which are common to its occurrence in a variety of contexts and which somehow make up its underlying subjective character. What Levinas does, in opposition to this, is to return to a position closer to, but more general than, Heidegger's account of what it is like to deal with things ready-to-hand, in particular, when things are not as we expect them to be, and this comes out in how we react.

Thus Levinas is sceptical of the kind of references to artwork made by the later Merleau-Ponty, as well as by Lyotard, to throw light on our experiences, and in particular, on our experiences of alterity. For an artwork only ever presents an 'image', divorced from life. 'The truth of being', comments Levinas sternly, 'is not the image of being.'[42] Indeed, Levinas's strictures are more general than already indicated. 'The proscription of images', he writes, 'is truly the supreme commandment of monotheism.'[43] While this no doubt reflects Levinas's Judaic background, it should not be read in a purely theological sense. It conveys a warning later echoed in Luce Irigaray's complaint that Merleau-Ponty, and, indeed, a whole masculine tradition 'privileges vision', but, perhaps more generally, a warning against a restricted use of the imagination for tackling problems about the character of an experience. For this has led, in Anglo-American philosophy, to a concentration on certain examples of the appearances of objects in the world of our activity.

As we shall see in the following chapter, the imagination is much more than a faculty for forming images. But thinking of it uncritically in this way can adversely affect the *philosophical* use of the imagination in considering what it is like to have certain sorts of experience and how those experiences relate one to things beyond. For, arguably, traditional approaches to these problems, and, perhaps, I have just suggested, much more recent ones, are vitiated by this dependence upon the formation of images of the contents of experience and a reading off of their properties, a tendency exacerbated by overreliance on examples of visual experience removed from their living contexts. Heidegger, the earlier Merleau-Ponty and Levinas counter this tendency with examples that do not so readily lend themselves to this restricted use of the imagination, yet which require us to think ourselves into the bodies of the subjects of experience: to rehearse their movements and to project the activities in which they will engage. This too, of course, is an exercise of imagination, but not one that involves the formation of images. Rather it requires looking past the experience itself to the role it plays in its subject's embodied existence in the world she faces, and faces with others who inhabit that world.

Summary

The problem which confronts accounts of experience like those of Heidegger and the early Merleau-Ponty is that, in rejecting 'contents' of experience which are given prior to conceptualisation, they fail to capture the way that experiences are something over and above what we make of them in treating them as reasons for action. For they are only that because they somehow exceed their role in our purposive activity by revealing a world in which this activity is not just successful or unsuccessful, but a response to something beyond its subject which, through experience, controls her acts. This problem of how experience can possibly point to something beyond itself in giving us reasons for action continues to preoccupy philosophers, like McDowell. Yet the later Merleau-Ponty, Lyotard and Levinas have already confronted it and offered a number of fruitful suggestions on how to resolve it.

The later Merleau-Ponty develops a notion of the 'flesh' as the common element between the subject and object of experience, drawing upon the fact that it is through the body that things act upon us, so that our bodies can be both subject and object, as when we touch ourselves. We can, perhaps, reinterpret this suggestion in terms of an appeal to the body as a causal mechanism whose operation can nonetheless provide us with reasons, rather than merely stimuli, because we each feel the effects of things on the body in the same way, and, consequently, as making our reactions intelligible. Thus what may seem from an observer's standpoint purely causal, a shared subjective viewpoint can reveal as being rational, and yet involving a response to what is other than ourselves, rather than to a merely internal happening.

Lyotard regards Merleau-Ponty as having failed to account for the 'event' to which we do respond in experience. His own suggestion is that we should attend to the indeterminate features of experience, prior to focusing on something and making it the intentional object of our awareness. This indeterminacy always exceeds any such determination in potentially grounding other judgements or producing other bodily reactions. It is this fact which shows that what we here experience is something other than anything we bring to it, and is, indeed, the 'event' revealed in all experience, which must start from such indeterminacy.

Levinas had earlier investigated states even less connected with the conceptualisation of objects of experience, for example, the experience of physical suffering. Paradoxically he finds that even here we are responding to something other than ourselves, for we are passive in the face of what assails us, and our bodily reactions are wrung out of us involuntarily. It is these reactions which, Levinas holds (like Wittgenstein), are basic to our life in the world, prior to any engaged activity in it, and which reveal something beyond us to which we are reacting. Again, as for Merleau-Ponty, it is the sharing of reactions which renders experience intelligible; so that 'things acquire a rational significance, and not only one of simple usage, because an other is associated with my relations with them'.[44] And Levinas thinks of these relations as founded on reactions to another's suffering or enjoyment. It is, again, the involuntariness of bodily reactions which forms the basis of the more complex control of thought by our experience of what is other than ourselves.

Notes

1. John McDowell, *Mind and World* (Cambridge, MA: Harvard University Press, 1994).
2. Ibid., pp. 9–10.
3. Ibid., p. 61.
4. Ibid., pp. 21–2.
5. David Farrell Krell (ed.), *Martin Heidegger: Basic Writings* (London: Routledge & Kegan Paul, 1978), p. 229.
6. Maurice Merleau-Ponty, 'The Intertwining – the Chiasm' (1961: one of Merleau-Ponty's final essays), reprinted Clive Cazeaux (ed.), *The Continental Aesthetics Reader* (London: Routledge, 2000), pp. 164–5.
7. Ibid., pp. 165–6.
8. Ibid., p. 165.
9. Ibid., p. 174.
10. Ibid., p. 170.
11. Ibid., pp. 173, 178, 172.

12. Jacques Lacan, *Four Fundamental Concepts of Psycho-analysis* (Harmondsworth: Penguin, 1977), p. 75.
13. Merleau-Ponty, 'Intertwining', p. 166.
14. Ibid., p. 167.
15. Ibid., p. 167.
16. Ibid., pp. 171–2.
17. See note 1.
18. Jean-François Lyotard, *Discours, Figure* (Paris: Klincksieck, 1971), p. 11.
19. Ibid., pp. 74–5.
20. Emmanuel Levinas, 'Ethics as First Philosophy', in Sean Hand (ed.), *The Levinas Reader* (Oxford: Blackwell, 1989), p. 79.
21. Lyotard, *Discours*, pp. 158–9.
22. Ibid., p. 239.
23. Immanuel Kant, *Kant's Critique of Aesthetic Judgement* (Oxford: Clarendon Press, 1911), §57.
24. Emmanuel Levinas, *Existence and Existents* (Hague: Nijhoff, 1978), pp. 98, 96.
25. Emmanuel Levinas, 'There Is: Existence without Existents', in Hand (ed.), *Levinas Reader*, p. 32.
26. Emmanuel Levinas, *Time and the Other* (Pittsburgh: Duquesne University Press, 1985), p. 46.
27. Emmanuel Levinas, *Otherwise than Being or beyond Essence* (Hague: Nijhoff, 1981), p. 63.
28. Emmanuel Levinas, 'Ethics as First Philosophy', in Hand (ed.), *Levinas Reader*, p. 80.
29. Emmanuel Levinas, 'Useless Suffering', in Robert Bernasconi and David Wood (eds), *The Provocation of Levinas* (London: Routledge, 1988), p. 157.
30. Ibid., pp. 159–60.
31. Ibid., p. 156.
32. Kant, *Kant's Critique of Aesthetic Judgement*, VII.
33. Quoted Jill Robbins, *Altered Readings* (Chicago: University of Chicago Press, 1999), p. 115.
34. Levinas, 'Useless Suffering', p. 158.
35. Ibid., p. 157.
36. Emmanuel Levinas, *Totality and Infinity* (Pittsburgh: Duquesne University Press, 1969), pp. 109–15.
37. Ibid., pp. 135–7.
38. Ibid., p. 130.
39. Ibid., p. 129.
40. Ibid., pp. 164–5.
41. It should not be thought, however, that these primitive bodily reactions are in some way fixed, and do not share the openness of the cognitive responses which is the mark of the excessiveness that characterises the exteriority of the events they record.
42. Levinas, *Totality and Infinity*, p. 291.
43. Quoted Robbins, *Altered Readings*, pp. 40–1.
44. Levinas, *Totality and Infinity*, p. 209.

3

Imagination and the Imaginary

Introduction

In much contemporary work there has been a shift from a conception of the imagination to explorations of the imaginary (or imaginaries).[1] In this chapter we want to explore the move from imagination, conceived of as some kind of faculty, perhaps that of creating inner or outer images, to the notion of the imaginary. We will suggest that the world, the experiences of which constitute our subjectivity, is an imaginary world and that the embodiment which constitutes our mode of being in that world is an imaginary embodiment. Here the notion of imaginary existence is not, as in many theories of the imagination, to be contrasted with the real, but rather to be taken as the condition for there being a real for us. The concept of the imaginary is offered as a conceptual resource for understanding our embodied subjectivity by interweaving the cognitive and affective forms which our worlds have for us.

Imagination and Perception

There is a tradition of thought regarding perception, deriving from Kant, discoverable in Wittgenstein, and highlighted in work by both Strawson[2] and Mary Warnock,[3] which signals the working of the imagination in perception. Here the suggestion is *not* that perception consists of inner images, representing the object perceived, and judged by the degree to which they match. Such a view maintains a distinction between the imagined object and the real object, which the accounts we have in mind wish to undermine. In contrast they see the imagination at work in the object of perception, not in some inner realm running parallel to it.

For Kant perceptual experience is not a passive process whereby impressions are received. It involves the active bringing to bear of concepts to sensations, which requires the activities of the imagination.

> What is first given to us is appearances. When combined with consciousness it is called perception. Now since every appearance contains a manifold, and since different perceptions therefore occur in the mind separately and singly, combination of them such as they cannot have in sense is demanded. There therefore must exist in us an active faculty for the synthesis of this manifold. To this faculty I give the name Imagination.[4]

Kant makes a distinction between the transcendental and empirical imagination. The transcendental imagination has a constructive role. It determines the forms of experiences in line with a priori concepts, rules, schemata which are necessary if we are to have experiences at all. In contrast the empirical imagination is not determined a priori. The particular empirical features in terms of which we organise our world are contingent and variable, a matter which can be explained by empirical laws of association. Both kinds of imagination are required if the chaos of sensory intuitions are to be brought to an order that can be experienced. Reflecting on this account one writer comments: 'Taking one's sensations as perceptions ... of a dog is, apparently, treated by Kant as analogous to the child's playfully seeing a broom as a horse.'[5] The same kind of activity is required of the subject in both cases, though the parallel is in no way meant to suggest that in the former case we are dealing with something illusory. The imagination is not linked to fantasy or chaos but rather to that which takes us beyond them.

The working of the imagination, which Kant suggests is present in everyday perceptions, as well as what would more readily be recognised as imaginative creations, is illustrated in an example of Sartre's. Sartre discusses the performance of a clown, Franconay, who is imitating Maurice Chevalier. At first the audience recognises that this is the person she is intending to imitate, perhaps via certain markers such as the hat and the cane. She remains, however, a small and plump woman imitating a man. But, as the performance continues, the audience becomes drawn into it. They begin to perceive her *as* Chevalier. 'We do not concentrate on the actual qualities of what we see. They are all incorporated into the object which we are beginning to imagine.'[6] Here is an explicit example of the workings of our imagination in the object. For Kant such examples are continuous with, rather than of a different order from, everyday perceptions. The imagination works by unifying a manifold, giving it a structure or form.

Strawson draws a comparison between Kant's account here and Wittgenstein's discussion of seeing as an aspect of perception, seeing the striking case of the change of aspect as 'merely dramatising a feature (namely seeing as) ... which is present in perception in general'.[7] He points to Wittgenstein's account of recognising a face. 'I meet someone whom I have not seen for years. I see him clearly, but fail to know him. Suddenly I know him. I see the old face in the altered one.'[8] Strawson emphasises continuity in the workings of imagination from

> seeing a cloud as a camel or a formation of stalagmites as a dragon ... to the first application of the word 'astringent' to a remark ... to a scientist seeing a pattern in phenomena which has never been seen before ... to Blake seeing eternity in a grain of sand and heaven in a wild flower.[9]

The imaginary forms which are at work here are, of course, reflected in the patterns of conceptualisation which our perceptual experiences bear. They do not, however, require explicit articulation. In the familiar negotiation of our environment, which Merleau-Ponty drew attention to as constitutive of perceptual experience for us,[10] finding our way around a room, picking up objects, negotiating obstacles, we are not necessarily engaged in explicit conceptualisation. Nonetheless we are operating with a practical imaginary in which our environment is experienced as having a certain shape or form.

From Imagination to the Imaginary

Many authors have recognised a particularly close link between imagination and emotion. Hume says, 'It is remarkable that the imagination and affections have a close union together, and that nothing that affects the former can be entirely indifferent to the latter.'[11] For Hume this link between imagination and passion appears contingent. It is simply a regularity which he has noticed. To recognise the imaginary dimension of experience as *constitutively* the domain of affect we need to turn to the use of that term by psychoanalytic thinkers.

Within psychoanalytic work the imaginary dimension is the realm of phantasy. For Freud phantasy provided us with a mode of representation of ourselves, our biological processes, our relationships to the world and others which was not governed by 'the reality principle' and considerations of truth and falsity, but by the demands of affect and emotion. The content of such phantasies reveals the emotional structure of the agent's world. In Freud's famous example of the Rat Man, the man had a recurrent dream in which he imagined his father had hungry rats on his bottom, which ate their way into his body. Also for this man rats served as an expression of hostility. When enraged he wished the rats on people. Despite the man's insistence that his father and he were the best of friends the process of analysis uncovered deep terror of a father who had punished him and on whom he wished back a fearful punishment.[12]

What is important to recognise here is that the content of such phantasmatic representations, the images and patterns which make them up, are the *vehicles* whereby the emotional contours of the subject's world become constituted. The relation between the affect and the phantasy is not simply one of causality but one of constitution. The images within phantasmatic representation carry the affects. Within certain of Freud's writings he 'sets the internal world, tending towards satisfaction by means of illusion, against an outside world which gradually imposes the reality principle'.[13] In other writings, however, he refers to '*psychical* reality', as a particular form of existence, an 'imaginary expression' of the instinctual dynamic.[14] For Freud these phantasmatic representations of the world operate at conscious and preconscious levels, but are frequently unconscious. They do, however, have effects in our life, underpinning and often disrupting the judgements of the conscious and apparently rational ego. 'These unconscious (mis)-representations can coexist in the mind with the knowledge acquired at a later stage, providing an affective substratum which determines a person's feelings (often unconscious) towards that later knowledge.'[15] Consequently:

> even aspects of behaviour that are far removed from imaginative activity and which appear at first glance to be governed solely by the demands of reality, emerge as ... derivatives of unconscious phantasy ... it is the subject's life as a whole which is seen to be shaped and ordered by what might be called ... a *phantasmatic*.[16]

For Freud the formation of the unconscious and the form of these phantasmatic representations were a part of the development of individual psyches (although they shared some universal features). They were a mode in which the emotional dynamics of personal relationships within the family and with significant others in later life were negotiated.

Lacan developed Freud's ideas by explicitly viewing the Imaginary as a stage (moment) in the development of the ego, a moment which then remains in play in later life. Lacan's key ideas here were developed in the paper 'The Mirror Stage as Formative of the "I", as Revealed in Psychoanalytic Experience'.[17] The mirror stage is the stage of development in which a baby first sees itself in a mirror and becomes fixated with that image. Gradually and jubilantly the child comes to view the image in the mirror as an image of itself. This is the first stage in the child's development of a sense of self, independent of other objects in the world. Although Lacan, in telling this story, discusses the child's relation to an actual mirror, it becomes clear that the identification of the child with an image of itself as a unified object distinct from other objects in the world, can be achieved by its relations with others who reflect back to the child the image which they have of it. For Lacan, the act of identification is a manifestation of affect. It is an emotional act, not a cognitive judgement. It is joyful and jubilant (and at other times aggressive and angry). These emotions are expressed by means of the child's relation to the image. Such moments of imaginary identification persist throughout our lives as vehicles of affective phantasy. The imaginary domain, governed by affect, pleasure, emotional conflict etc. remains as a dimension of adult identity. These imaginary identifications, as with Freud's phantasies, frame our relations to the world.

For Lacan, however, the image with which the child identifies is something *outside itself*, an image or a reflection of itself back from another. This external object then becomes internalised as a sense of self. The *imaginary self* which the child develops in this way is, however, for Lacan necessarily *illusory*. It sits in tension with the child's sensory sense of its bodily existence which is still multiple and fragmented. Ultimately such an imaginary identification is a source of error and falsehood. These imaginary identifications frame our relations to the world in a way that, for Lacan, because of their illusory nature, were ultimately futile. In this account because of the emphasis on the imaginary world as an illusion (though one with real effects) Lacan appears to retain a contrast, found in some work on the imagination, between the imaginary and the real. In Lacan's framework, however, we cannot be rescued from the illusions of the imaginary by attention to the Real. The Real for Lacan is necessarily unarticulable, unrepresentable and undifferentiated. It lies outside of signification as the realm of impossible plenitude and bliss. There is no way back to this for those who are subjects. Its pursuit leads only to psychosis. Lacan instead suggests that the route out of imaginary illusion is through the Symbolic. Following the mirror stage comes the ongoing process of becoming subjects via subjection to the Symbolic order which is formed by language. Language, for Lacan, as for Saussure,[18] is already there, as a publicly and socially given structure. Our psychic processes are formed from the structures of such language. Also, Lacan, following Saussure, resists an account in which the meaning of language is given by its correspondence with things, insisting instead on the autonomy of language. 'Language must be viewed as a system of structural relations that precedes and is presupposed by any given utterance.' It is an internally related system of sound *differences* or 'binary oppositions' which make meaning possible in the first place. Our psychic processes are formed from the structures of such language. We become subjects by inserting ourselves into an already existing Symbolic order. 'We remain oblivious while making things with words of the extent to which words make us.'[19] We gain access to our psychic structures and thereby to ourselves as subjects by attending to the structures of language. Any search for a word-free thought underneath language is an impossible and incoherent quest. Language both imprisons and liberates us. It forces us to abandon the passionate world of the Imaginary but is necessary if we are to function as subjects and agents. It offers the (apparent) possibility of rationality, coherence and objectivity, and, importantly, movement and change. The role of psychoanalysis, for Lacan, should be to release desire from the grip of the Imaginary and into the intersubjective and social world of the Symbolic order.

In Lacan, then, we have an account of the Imaginary which establishes its constitutive link to affect, but apparently at the cost of tying the imaginary realm to illusion, a world we must sacrifice to the social world of language . In Lacan the specular images, which carry the affective realm of the Imaginary, are contrasted to the linguistic structures governing the Symbolic. But such a division seems forced. Other writers have challenged the clear division between the imaginary and the Symbolic, which Lacan is keen to guard. The Symbolic has embedded in it an imaginary order. As Castoriadis expresses it, language is not only a *code*, 'a quasi-univocal instrument of making/doing, reckoning and elementary reasoning. The code aspect of language (the cat is on the mat) is opposed to but also inextricably entangled with its poetic aspects, carrying the imaginary significations'.[20] The Symbolic is not reduced narrowly to the realm of language. It includes myth, stories and artifacts and non-linguistic practices with imaginary attachments. The French philosopher and psychoanalyst Luce Irigaray has been particularly concerned with the imaginary of the female body and the concept 'woman' as it was manifest in both philosophical and psychoanalytic thought and the wider cultural setting. For Irigaray 'the feminine finds itself defined as lack, deficiency'.[21] The position which Irigarary is drawing our attention to here is, interdependently, a position within language and a structure within our affective responses. 'she functions as a hole, in the elaboration of imaginary and Symbolic processes.'[22] In opposition to Lacan, but in common with Castoriadis, she saw the imaginary as intertwined with a Symbolic. The imaginary is structured by the Symbolic as well as constituting its affective dimension. The images, forms, in the extended sense in which we have come to use that term in this chapter, carry the affect.

In rejecting the division between the imaginary and the Symbolic, the imaginary is no longer cast as necessarily illusory. Instead we can marry the Strawsonian conception of the imagination, as the condition of there being a real for us, with the psychoanalytic conception of the imaginary. In consequence the imaginary forms, which are constitutive of our experience of the world, are the bearers of affective significance, the means by which we not only think but also feel our way around that world. The images carry our affective relations to our world and each other. Nicole Brossard writes,

> The image is a vital resource that forms complex propositions from simple and isolated elements. Each time an image relays desire, this image thinks, with unsuspected vitality, the drift of meaning. So it is that images penetrate the solid matter of our ideas.[23]

The world which we encounter is therefore an imaginary world. It is a world of which we strive to make not only cognitive but also affective sense. The sense, which it makes for us, is carried by the images which constitute its form. Here, following Heidegger, we must beware of a certain picture. It is not the case that we perceive some neutral world and project onto it some imaginary significance derived from our inner feelings.

> We do not, so to speak, throw a 'signification' over some naked thing which is present-at-hand, we do not stick a value on it; but when something within-the-world is encountered as such, the thing in question already has an involvement which is disclosed in our understanding of the world.[24]

On this account the world we encounter already has an imaginary form, which yields the affective significance which it has for us.

Social Imaginaries

Within the psychoanalytic accounts of the imaginary, imaginary identifications are prompted by psychic mechanisms. The jubilation the infant expresses in relation to its mirror image appears internally prompted, even while it is a manifestation of a stage of development which is viewed as universal. Further and distinctive imaginary investments are accounted for in terms of an individual's personal history. Nonetheless the images, which for Lacan are the vehicle of psychic identifications, are provided by the social context in which we are anchored. Lacan's later seminars replace the mirror image with reference to the screen with its clear overtones of a socially constructed content.[25] However, for Lacan, the intervention of the social comes decisively with the entry into the Symbolic, when the narcissistic and phantasmatic formation of the ego has to be set aside, in order that a socially recognisable subject can emerge capable of effective agency within the social world.

Once a rigid division between the imaginary and Symbolic realms is rejected then it is clear that imaginary investments, at least in part, are an outcome of social processes. We are initiated into the imaginary significance of our world in being initiated into the Symbolic order. For Castoriadis the imagination has two key connotations, first, its connections with images, 'in the most general sense of forms'[26] and, secondly, its connection with creation. His primary concern is with the 'radical imagination' in both its individual and social manifestation. This radical imagination is 'what makes it possible for any being-for-itself to *create for* itself an own world ... within which it also posits itself'.[27] This imagination is *before* the distinction between 'real' and 'fictitious'.[28] The imagination is therefore not set up in opposition to the real, but inheres in both the real and the fictitious. There are clear parallels here with Kant (although Castoriadis berates Kant for tying imagination too closely to the laws of the understanding). In the operation of this imagination, to create a world, Castoriadis describes a process in which the individual and the social radical imaginaries are mutually interdependent, without either being reducible to the other. The radical imagination is something which we all possess as individuals and without which there could be no world for us. He also accepts the elements of a psychoanalytic picture in which emotional investments and the imaginaries in which they find expression reflect both inner processes and personal histories.

> [But] the psyche ... has to abandon more or less its own world, its objects of investment, what is for it meaning, and to cathect socially created and valorised objects, orientations ... The institutions supply the psyche with meaning ... this is accomplished by the social imaginary significations.[29]

Such social imaginary significations can be very variable in different social settings. In this process, however, in which the psyche 'introjects' such shared imaginaries it also 'reinterprets' them. The resultant imaginary significations of our world consequently reflect both shared social imaginaries and individual life histories. The individual and social aspects of our imaginary worlds also open the possibilities of conflict between them, an issue which we will discuss more below.

The social 'imaginary is that which defines social identity ... gives unity to an incalculable number of gestures, investing the world with meaning, content and style'.[30] Genevieve Lloyd discusses the social imaginary in which white Australians thinking of their history imagine Australia as a *terra nullius* prior to British colonisation, an image conditioning their relation to their land, their past and their future, and crucially their relation to indigenous peoples. 'The founding fiction ...

was the "discovery" of a vast and … empty land … devoid of law and society and so without a history'.[31] The legal fiction of *terra nullius* was overturned in 1992. Paul Keating, then prime minister, in response, emphasises that non-indigenous Australians needed to change their ways of thinking. 'It was we who did the dispossessing. We took the traditional lands and smashed the traditional way of life … we committed the murders. We took the children from their mothers.'[32] Here Keating is not simply amassing facts . He is trying to bring about a change in the way the past is imagined, and consequently felt about. He is putting a different image or form on that past, which carries with it a different mode of feeling, and thereby acting in response to it.

Genevieve Lloyd, together with Moira Gatens, though using a concept of the imaginary very close to that of Castoriadis and Irigaray, acknowledges as her primary influence the work of Spinoza. What these writers derive from Spinoza is a concept of our imaginaries as 'affectively laden thought patterns',[33] which constitute our modes of being in the world and thereby constitute our subjectivity. 'Spinoza's account of the imagination is … a theory about a permanent structure through which human beings are constituted as such.'[34] For Spinoza the mind is a form of direct bodily awareness, an awareness of the environment and context which impinge on our bodies. The imagination is part of such awareness. Because each mind is the idea of a different body, with a different life history, there will be a divergence between different imaginary orders. These differences, however, will not be entirely individualistic. For our modes of being in the world, though variable, are inherently social. 'The affections of individual bodies', Spinoza holds, 'lay down widely divergent associational paths; from traces of a horse seen in the sand, the soldier passes to thought of horsemen and war, the farmer to ploughs and fields.'[35]

> But although these patterns are individual and idiosyncratic – multiple in contrast to the unitary order of reason – the variations are not a product of the affections of individual bodies in isolation from others. Farming and military activity give rise to different associational paths which reflect different practices.[36]

Different imaginaries are therefore tied up with different ways of responding to and acting in relation to our environment. They are constitutively linked to different practices and ways of life.

> The social imaginary is constitutive of, not merely reflective of, the forms of sociability in which we live. The imaginary endures through time and so becomes increasingly embedded in all our institutions, our judicial systems, our national narratives, our founding fictions, our cultural traditions.[37]

Imaginary Bodies

The affective constitution of our imaginary worlds carries a reflexive element. To view the world affectively is to register its possibilities for pleasure and pain. It opens the world for engagement, possibilities for our own becoming in relation to it. The content of our imaginary world is thereby made manifest in our actual and potential responsiveness to it. The salience and significance we see in our world is linked not causally but constitutively to the recognition of certain responses as appropriate to it, and this, as has been evident in previous chapters, to the holding of our bodies in readiness to respond. Genevieve Lloyd attributes to Spinoza the recognition that imagination is a 'form of bodily awareness',[38] in which the nature of other bodies of all kinds are imagined together with our own. Lloyd discusses Virginia Woolf's articulation of the 'fiction governing the interaction of men and women: [the image of] the "angel in the house"'. Here the image manifests itself in the woman's behaviour. 'If there is a chicken she takes a leg; if there is a draught she sits in it.'[39] Woolf's 'angel' sees the chicken leg as that which is for her to take, the draught as for her to sit in. The mode of perception is embodied in the mode of her response. The imaginary form which our world has is therefore interdependent with the imaginary forms of our own embodiment. A good of example of such an embodied imaginary is given by Mark Twain:

> Ben ... was eating an apple and giving a loud melodious whoop at intervals, followed by a deep toned ding-dong-dong, ding-dong-dong, for he was personating a steam boat! As he drew near he slackened speed, took the middle of the street, leaned far over to starboard, and rounded to ponderously ... the headway ran almost out and he drew up slowly towards the sidewalk. 'Ship up to back! Ting-a-ling-ling!' His arms straightened and stiffened down his sides ... His right hand meantime describing stately circles – for it was representing a forty foot wheel. 'Let her go back on the labboard! Ting-a-ling-ling! Chow-ch-chow-chow!' The left hand began to describe circles ... Tom went on whitewashing – paid no attention to the steamer.[40]

Our bodily modes of engaging with our world capture the imaginary form which those worlds have for us. The interdependence of the imaginary forms of our world with the nature of actual and potential bodily responses means that the process of social initiation into our shared imaginary worlds is often a process of bodily training ('Sit up straight when your father is talking to you!'). This is a process to which we will pay attention in Chapter 6.

Imaginary worlds therefore require imaginary bodies. Embodiment is our mode of being in the world. As we saw in Chapter 1 and discuss further in Chapter 6 below, this body in the world is an intentional body, apt for or engaged in projects. The mode in which our bodies inhabit the world is shown in habitual action. The body simply responds appropriately to the world by means of intentional acts: for example, opening doors, picking up objects, scratching our nose, typing, playing an instrument. All of these activities, as noted above, require a practical imaginary of the environment we are in. They also require some kind of awareness of our bodies as having a certain shape or form, a shape or form which is constituted interdependently with the forms which we find in our worlds. In Chapter 1 we referred to Merleau-Ponty's conception of 'body image', in terms of our ability to know, pre-reflectively, where the parts of our body are in relation to each other and things in our vicinity. For Merleau-Ponty body image is 'a total awareness of my posture in the intersensory world, a form in the sense used by Gestalt psychology'.[41] Such a form is 'neither the mere copy nor even the global awareness of the existing parts of the body', but the integration of these in relation to 'the organism's projects'.[42] Iris Marion Young cites as an example of such awareness a passage from a short story 'describing a kitchen dance in which a farm woman cans her tomatoes while mindful of the colicky baby she holds between her arm and her hip'.[43] Such actions require a *corporeal or postural schema* or *body image* which is manifest in our actions and responses and makes them possible.

In order to draw a distinction between the body image and the anatomical or biological body Merleau-Ponty focuses on cases of phantom limbs, where a subject retains a body image and consequent habitual dispositions even when the body as characterised by biology lacks the appropriate limb. (Having a breast removed, for example, can leave one repeatedly attempting to rest ones arm in an empty space.) 'To have a phantom arm is to remain open to all the actions of which the arm alone is capable; it is to retain the practical field which one enjoyed before mutilation.'[44] On this account our mode of experiencing our bodies is not brute or unmediated. Our postural schemas or body images are already *morphologies*, that is, mediated forms of organisation, not simply brute causal responses to anatomical shape. A danger here is that the concept of body image can suggest something like an inner mental map or picture which we have of our bodies. This separates the image from what it is supposed to be an image of. It makes the image a mental representation of the body. However, it is more accurate to think of our body images as the form of our bodies, in a way that parallels the operation of the imagination in perception, as discussed in the first section of this chapter. For Merleau-Ponty the body image is interdependent with our imagining of the world. Body and world form a unified gestalt, in which the body is experienced as a potentiality for action in the world, and the world as a world of possibility for the body.

It is not only as such a unified gestalt, however, that the body image enters into the formation of our subjectivity. It was emphasised in the discussion above that imaginary forms are the carriers of affect, and this is equally true of imagined bodily forms. The psychologist Paul Schilder, for example, remarks, regarding phantom limbs, 'the phantom of an amputated person is ... the reactivation of a given perceptive pattern by emotional forces. The great variety in phantoms is only to be understood when we consider the emotional reactions of individuals towards their own bodies.'[45] Schilder emphasises the role of phantasy in the construction of body image, and consequently the multiplicity that we have of such images: 'We let it [the postural model of the body] shrink playfully, and come to the idea of Lilliputians, or we transform it into giants.'[46] The role of affect and phantasy in the formation of bodily image links, for Schilder, to the affective interactions we have with others: 'The touches of others, the interest others take in the different parts of the body, will be of enormous importance in the development of the postural schema of the body'.[47] The way we have of imagining our bodies and those of others therefore invests particular contours with emotional and affective salience.

The bodily image which is being described here is not simply giving affective form to one object among others in the world, even if that one is necessary for the delivery of our projects in the world. The body is constitutively what is recognised as the self, the *moi*, the ego. The imaginary forms of our bodies therefore constitute our sense of ourselves. Schilder is, of course, building on the work of Freud, who claimed that 'the ego is first and foremost a bodily ego'.[48] What Freud is drawing attention to here is that our sense of self is a sense of a body and involves an awareness of that body as having a certain shape or form. But, for Freud, the contours of the body are structured by emotion and desire (the ensuing bodily image is therefore not something which could be captured simply by the drawing of a picture). It is not that an already structured anatomical body produces our sense of it, our body image. Rather the body becomes formed by being invested with affect. In 'On Narcissism' and *The Ego and the Id* Freud discussed pain.[49] In the first of these texts, highlighting the libidinal investment in the pain of toothache, he quotes, 'concentrated is his soul ... in his molar's aching hole'.[50] In the later text, discussing the formation of the ego, he claims:

Pain seems to play a part in this process, and the way in which we gain new knowledge of our organs during painful illness is, perhaps, the model of the way by which, in general, we arrive at the idea of our own body.[51]

As Judith Butler points out:

in a significant sense that body part does not exist for consciousness prior to that investiture, indeed that body part is delineated and becomes knowable for Freud only on the condition of that investiture ... As a result, it would not be possible to speak about a body part that precedes and gives rise to an idea, for it is the idea that emerges simultaneously with the phenomenologically accessible body, indeed that guarantees its accessibility ... Freud ... confirms here the indissolubility of a body part and the phantasmatic partitioning that brings it into psychic experience.[52]

Some of our bodily zones and shapes become significant to us, while others are barely noticed.

The significance Freud places on bodily sensations in forming the contours of the imaginary body, which constitutes the ego, is in contrast to the overarching role which is played in Lacan by the mirror image, and later the screen, in the formation of the bodily ego. Here the sense of self is achieved by what is a *misidentification* with an external image. Although this external image sits in some tension with the sensational body, experienced as 'the body in bits and pieces',[53] it offers the sense of a coherent whole, the jubilant relation with which initiates the ego, a sense of *moi*, as opposed to other objects in the world. Other writers, however, in discussing the child's relation to the image in the mirror tell a somewhat different story. The psychologist Wallon[54] sees the child spending a period of time integrating the perceived image with the sense of itself derived from proprioception. The image in the mirror is for some time experienced as the self, *over there*, at a distance from the sensationally experienced body. When integration occurs it is less the misrecognition of an external object as self and more a form incorporated into the sensational body. The wholeness or coherence which results is for Wallon and the psychologist Schilder always precarious.[55]

In the terms of Moira Gatens, the imaginary body is:

the social and personal significance of the body as lived ... The imaginary body is socially and historically specific in that it is constructed by: a shared language; the shared psychical significance and privileging of various zones of the body; and common institutional practices and discourses (for example, medical, juridical and educational).[56]

The imaginary body formed from individual engagements and personal histories confronts images of the body reflected back to us from our social environment. Such images become incorporated into the corporeal forms which make possible our intentional engagement with our imaginary worlds. The way the body is experienced reflects responses to it from within families, as well as those which are found in public images and writings. The consequence is that our body feels to us in such a way that it makes possible certain kinds of agency and inhibits others. As Iris Marion Young has illustrated, such incorporation mediates even the way in which boys and girls throw balls, walk, sit on seats etc.[57] In *The Second Sex* Simone de Beauvoir gives an account of the young girl's experience of her body as she reaches puberty.

> At about the age of twelve or thirteen ... the crisis begins ... when the breasts and body hair are developing ... she inspects herself with ... astonishment and horror ... the enlargement of this ... painful core, appearing under each nipple ... this new growth in her armpits and middle transforms her into a kind of animal or alga.[58]

Sexual difference, within such a framework, is constituted out of the imaginary investments in different bodily parts. The same is true of other aspects of bodily identity. As Linda Alcoff points out, raced identity derives from the affective investments in bodily parts, shape of nose, or colour of skin, which bring them into play as part of the contour or form constituting the body as imagined.[59] It is such imagined bodies that form the basis of the distinctions in terms of which we then negotiate our world. The body, as it features in these accounts, is a body experienced not only cognitively but also affectively. That is, not only do we categorise the bodies of ourselves and others but also we imagine them in ways which structure the possibility of response.

Given that particular bodies have individual histories, even when lived within a shared social space, we can understand both shared bodily imaginaries and individual differences also. These differences will be the result of particular familial and other emotional and desiring engagements, which particular bodies have undergone and which inform the way in which those bodies are experienced as significant. This concept of the imaginary therefore goes some way to explaining both similarities and differences in our modes of experiencing our bodies.

Given the different sources of the imaginary forms which constitute the embodied self, space opens up for tensions between them, threatening the (albeit illusory) unity which for Lacan founds the ego. The specular image, reflected back by others on the screen, can conflict with the corporeal schema, informed by sensations of pleasure and pain, which ground our intentional negotiations of our world. Moreover there are multiple screens and a variety of relations with significant others reflecting back to us different imaginaries in terms of which our bodies can be constituted. In many cases there is a severe disjuncture between prior individual body image or corporeal posture, enabling habitual and unconscious negotiation of their world, and the social salience which we discover our bodies, and thereby our worlds, to have. Kaja Silverman invokes the accounts of Fanon, describing his experiences on arriving in France and discovering the imaginary significance which his body has for others.

> Assailed at various points [my pre-existing] corporeal schema crumbles. I [subject] myself to an objective examination, I [discover] my blackness, my ethnic characteristics; and I [am] battered down by tom-toms, cannibalism, intellectual deficiency, fetishism, racial defects, slave ships and above all 'sho'good eating'.

As Silverman makes clear:

> [T]he struggle here is not to close the distance between visual imago and the proprioceptive body, as in the classic account of identification, but to maintain it – to keep the screen of 'blackness' at a safe remove from the sensational ego, lest it assume precisely that quality of self sameness which is synonymous with a coherent ego … Fanon finds himself occupying not one point in space, but two or three.[60]

Changing Imaginaries

De Beauvoir sees the girl's way of experiencing her body as, given the society in which she lives, inevitable. The possibility of her participation in public life therefore requires her to transcend her body, distance her subjectivity from it to develop a sense of self in despite of its messy embodiment. Such a denial, she also recognised, carried with it emotional cost. The sense that transformation of imaginary investments is not possible might also be informing the decisions of transsexuals (and others) to change their bodies. The interdependent body/world imaginaries, constituting their sense of self and making possible intentional agency, cannot be married to the social salience which it is found particular bodily forms carry. For Fanon the struggle was to keep his own body image, which enabled him to operate intentionally in the world, *separate* from the damaging social imaginings which he encountered. The struggle here is not to let the awareness of how his body is experienced by others become part of his own experiences of it.

Spinoza, along with other writers we have been discussing, notes that the imagination has a logic of its own, and has a resilience which can result in its persistence even when challenged by claims of truth or falsity: 'No affect can be restrained by the true knowledge of good and evil insofar as it is true, but only insofar as it is considered as an affect.'[61] We cannot, for example, modify damaging representations of women simply by claiming they are false (women too can reason or carry heavy weights). For the way women are imagined, the response of men (and women) to female bodies will not necessarily be changed. Moira Gatens gives a good illustration of this point in her discussion of the attitudes of judges and jurors in rape trials. Judges and jurors are subject to training which instructs them that neither a woman's sexual history nor her trustworthiness can be gauged from her appearance. If asked to express their beliefs on this matter, many would express just that. Nonetheless their responses to witnesses as trustworthy or provocative can remain in an imaginary realm governed by both social imaginaries and individual histories.[62] Pointing out that there were people in Australia when British settlers arrived can have bearing on the image of *terra nullius*. But it is not sufficient. To dislodge this image those people and their social arrangements and relationships to the land have to be imagined in ways that give them rights over its use and disposition.

Nonetheless Spinoza thought it was possible to reflect rationally on the workings of the imagination. The patterns of associations which were generated by specific images could be made a subject of scrutiny. Moreover, 'he sees these organised pattern of affect and image as changeable through challenging the appropriateness of the images at their core'. In this way we can 'learn to replace misleading and debilitating illusions with better fictions'.[63] Our imaginary worlds are perspectival. They are worlds from the perspective of embodied subjectivities whose corporeal forms, personal histories and social and cultural anchorage are implicated in the imaginary forms which their worlds possess. They are not, however, private. Imaginary significations carry an implicit publicness and are therefore susceptible to some processes of evaluation. Others who can grasp the context should be able to grasp the imaginary form as a possible one. This process, however, is not that of checking an independently accessible reality to see if the representation of it is accurate. It is more like seeing if the world and subject can carry the signification suggested. The process of forming and changing imaginary significations is a creative one. What we are offered has to make both affective and not just cognitive sense to us. It must change our modes of experiencing our worlds in ways that we can recognise as desirable and livable.

Jeanette Winterson's heroine in *The Powerbook* tells her lover stories of old romances.[64] If we adopted the framework of the Lacanian

Imaginary she is projecting onto her relationship a phantasmatic and illusory image of the romantic couple, which can have no correspondence with the real. To remain psychically functional and able to act within a social world she must curb such phantasy and accommodate herself to the framework of sexual desire made possible in the social Symbolic. In rejecting this picture, by rejecting the Lacanian assimilation of the Imaginary with the illusory, we need not, however, place Winterson's imaginary configurations beyond scrutiny. However, her lover, or the reader, is not asked to judge whether the relationship between the lovers is properly represented by those stories. They have to be assessed in a different light. They are providing a structure or form in terms of which the affective relationship is to be conducted. Can the relationship bear (in the sense of carry) this form in a way that makes it livable for the couple concerned? Can the form make sense of their interactions with each other? Are there other ways of imagining their interactions which have a greater chance of a successful outcome?

Given the role of the imaginary, assessment as appropriate or inappropriate has to concern the confrontation of different ways of inhabiting our world and living affectively and effectively within it. For the writer bell hooks the project is to provide ways of reimagining black bodies in livable ways. To this end she attempts to link the diversity of contemporary black experience in America back to historical roots in a Southern black rural world. In this way the skin of the man lying next to her, 'soot black like my granddaddy's skin', can return her to 'a world where we had a history ... a world where ... something wonderful might be a ripe tomato, found as we walked through the rows of daddy Jerry's garden'.[65] hooks's reimagining here is a strategy also adopted by other feminist writers, with respect to the female body. Irigaray has been the most important influence here, insisting on the need to develop *different* imaginaries of the female body which would allow femininity to be lived in a less destructive way.[66] Unlike Lacan and like Castoriadis, Irigaray is claiming that such imaginary transformations can take place. It does, however, require creative work, the production of new images, which can take hold in people's lives. It only succeeds when people are faced with alternative images which 'grab their imagination', give them satisfying and livable ways of being in their environment.

Summary

In this chapter we have distilled a concept of the imaginary with which to make good the claim that our mode of embodied subjectivity is an imaginary embodiment in an imaginary world. The concept of the imaginary which we are employing is not one in which imaginary worlds are contrasted to real worlds. The imagined world is rather the form which we give to our corporeal bodies and our material world. Imagined worlds are not inner images projected onto a neutral world. A world can only be a world for us by means of the operation of the imagination. There is no neutral world to which we can gain access. The images and forms in terms of which our imagined worlds are constituted carry in an interdependent way both cognition and affects. Consequently the imagined relation is an affective relation to the world. To view the world affectively is not simply to see it as containing certain potentialities for actions but to see such actions as appropriate or desirable, invested with possibilities of pleasure and pain.

Our imaginary bodies and imaginary worlds are mutually constitutive. We imagine our bodies in terms of their potentiality for action which requires an imagined world. Moreover imagining the world in a certain way is to view it in terms of possibilities for *our* existence. Imagining the world is a mode of being in relation to it. Nonetheless these imagined worlds are not private. Where such imagined worlds are not illusory there is an implicit publicness to the forms they can take. The appropriateness of the imaginary form must be recognisable by those who can grasp the point of view.

The link between imaginary worlds and embodied points of view explains differences within different people's imaginary worlds and the same person's imaginary world at different (and sometimes the same) times. It must not, however, obscure the role of the social. First, our encounters with objects and significant others forms our imaginary embodiment through which our world gains its imaginary form. Second, through our participation in social groups we are initiated into social imaginaries which make possible shared responses to the world and consequently shared forms of life.

Imagined configurations have a resilience which makes their displacement more than a simple(!) matter of appealing to considerations of truth or falsity. Crucially it involves encounters with alternative imagined configurations, which can be recognised as making both cognitive and affective sense.

Notes

1. Here and throughout the chapter we will talk of the *imaginary* and *imaginaries*. We will restrict the term *Imaginary* for the Lacanian Imaginary alone.
2. P. Strawson, 'Imagination and Perception', in P. Strawson, *Freedom and Resentment and Other Essays* (London: Methuen, 1974).

3. M. Warnock, *Imagination* (London and Boston: Faber and Faber, 1976).

4. I. Kant, *Critique of Pure Reason*, trans. N. Kemp Smith (London: Macmillan, 1929), A120.

5. O'Leary Hawthorne, 'Imagination', in E. Craig (ed.), *Routledge Encyclopedia of Philosophy* (London: Routledge, 1998), p. 22.

6. Warnock, *Imagination*, p. 170.

7. Strawson, 'Imagination and Perception', p. 79.

8. L. Wittgenstein, *Philosophical Investigations*, trans. G. E. M. Anscombe (Oxford: Blackwell, 1953), p. 197.

9. Strawson, 'Imagination and Perception', p. 63.

10. For further discussion see Chapter 1 and Chapter 6.

11. D. Hume, *Treatise of Human Nature*, trans. L. A. Selby Bigge (Oxford: Oxford University Press, 1888), part III section 6.

12. S. Freud, 'Notes on a Case of Obsessional Neurosis', in S. Freud, *The Standard Edition of the Collected Psychological Works of Sigmund Freud*, trans. James Strachey (London: Hogarth Press, 1974), vol. X, pp. 153ff.

13. J. Laplanche and J.-B. Pontalis, *The Language of Psychoanalysis* (London: Karnac Books, 1973), p. 315.

14. Ibid., p. 315.

15. M. Whitford, *Luce Irigaray: Philosophy in the Feminine* (London and New York: Routledge, 1991), p. 64.

16. Laplanche and Pontalis, *Language of Psychoanalysis*, p. 317.

17. J. Lacan, 'The Mirror Stage as Formative of the "I", as Revealed in Psychoanalytic Experience', in J. Lacan, *Ecrits: A Selection*, trans. A. Sheridan (New York: Norton, 1977).

18. F. de Saussure, *Course in General Linguistics* (London: Duckworth, 1983).

19. Saussure, *Course in General Linguisitics*; selections reprinted in R. Kearney and M. Rainwater (eds), *The Continental Philosophy Reader* (London: Routledge, 1996), pp. 296–7.

20. C. Castoriadis, 'Radical Imagination and the Social Instituting Imaginary', in G. Robinson and J. Rundell (eds), *Rethinking Imagination* (London and New York: Routledge, 1994), p. 150.

21. Whitford, *Luce Irigaray*, p. 67.

22. Ibid., p. 66.

23. N. Brossard, 'Green Night of Labyrinth Park', in B. Warland (ed.), *Inversions: Writings by Dykes, Queers and Lesbians* (Vancouver: Press Gang Publishers, 1991), p. 196.

24. M. Heidegger, *Being and Time*, trans. J. Macquarrie and E. Robinson (Oxford: Blackwell, 1962), H 150.

25. J. Lacan, *Four Fundamental Concepts of Psychoanalysis*, trans. A. Sheridan (New York: Norton, 1978).

26. Castoriadis, 'Radical Imagination', p. 138.

27. Ibid., p. 143.

28. Ibid., p. 138.

29. Ibid., p. 150.

30. L. McNay, *Gender and Agency* (Oxford: Polity, 2000), p. 145.

31. M. Gatens and G. Lloyd, *Collective Imaginings* (London and New York: Routledge, 1999), p. 145.

32. Ibid., p. 142.

33. Ibid., p. 5.

34. Ibid., p. 142.

35. G. Lloyd, 'Spinoza and the Education of the Imagination', in A. Rorty (ed.), *Philosophers on Education* (London and New York: Routledge, 1998), p. 162.

36. Ibid.

37. Gatens and Lloyd, *Collective Imaginings*, p. 143.

38. Lloyd, 'Spinoza', p. 160.

39. Ibid., p. 170.

40. M. Twain, *The Adventures of Tom Sawyer* (London: Longman, 1965).

41. M. Merleau-Ponty, *Phenomenology of Perception*, trans. C. Smith (London: Routledge and Kegan Paul, 1962), p. 99.

42. Ibid.

43. I. Marion Young, 'Throwing like a Girl: Twenty Years Later', in D. Welton (ed.), *Body and Flesh: A Philosophical Reader* (Oxford: Blackwell, 1998), p. 21.

44. Merleau-Ponty, *Phenomenology of Perception*, p. 81.

45. P. Schilder, *The Image and Appearance of the Human Body: Studies in the Constructive Energies of the Psyche* (New York: International Universities Press, 1950), p. 67.

46. Ibid. See also discussion in G. Weiss, *Body Images: Embodiment as Intercorporeality* (New York and London: Routledge, 1999), Chapter 1.

47. Schilder, *Image and Appearance of the Human Body*, p. 126.

48. S. Freud, 'The Ego and the Id', in S. Freud, *The Standard Edition of the Complete Psychological Works of Sigmund Freud*, vol. XIX, trans. and ed. by James Strachey (London: Hogarth Press, 1961), p. 26.

49. S. Freud, 'On Narcissism: An Introduction', in Freud, *Standard Edition*, vol. XIX.

50. J. Butler, *Bodies That Matter* (New York and London: Routledge, 1993), p. 58.

51. Freud, 'The Ego and the Id', pp. 25–6.

52. Butler, *Bodies That Matter*, pp. 58–9.

53. J. Lacan, *The Seminar of Jacques Lacan*, book 1, trans. J. Forrester (Cambridge: Cambridge University Press, 1988).

54. H. Wallon, 'Kinesthesia and the Visual Body Image in the Child', in H. Wallon, *The World of Henri Wallon*, ed. G. Voyat (New York: Jason Aronson, 1984).

55. See the discussion of Wallon and Schilder in K. Silverman, *The Threshold of the Visible World* (London and New York: Routledge, 1996).

56. M. Gatens, *Imaginary Bodies* (London and New York: Routledge, 1996), p. 25.

57. I. Marion Young, 'Throwing like a Girl'.

58. S. de Beauvoir, *The Second Sex* (Harmondsworth: Penguin, 1982), p. 32.

59. L. Alcoff, 'Towards a Phenomenology of Racial Embodiment', *Radical Philosophy*, 95, 1999, pp. 15–22.

60. Fanin quoted and commented on in Silverman, *Threshold of the Visible World*, p. 28.

61. Lloyd, 'Spinoza', p. 168.

62. Gatens, *Imaginary Bodies*, p. 138.

63. Gatens and Lloyd, *Collective Imaginings*, p. 26.

64. J. Winterson, *The Powerbook* (London: Hutchinson, 2002).

65. b. hooks, *Feminist Theory: From Margin to Centre* (Boston, MA: South End Press, 1984), p. 30.

66. See M. Whitford (ed.), *The Irigaray Reader* (Oxford: Blackwells, 1992).

4

Desire

My mother's longing shaped my own childhood. From a Lancashire mill town and a working class twenties childhood she came away wanting; fine clothes, glamour, money; to be what she wasn't. However that longing was produced in her distant childhood, what she actually wanted were real things, real entities which she materially lacked, things that a culture and a social system withheld from her.[1]

Just because people ask you for something doesn't mean that's what they really want you to give them.[2]

Desire is intentional in that it is always desire of or for a given object or Other, but it is also reflexive in the sense that desire is a modality in which the subject is both discovered and enhanced.[3]

Depth and Surface

Within much contemporary analytic philosophy of mind desires are conceived of primarily as the inner states which provide us, together with beliefs, with reasons for forming intentions and consequently acting. When linked with beliefs, such desires then cause us to act in appropriate ways. Desires therefore have a role both in providing premises for practical reasoning and a causal, functional role in terms of the agent's behaviour. Weaving these two roles together has been one of the challenges of contemporary materialism. Within standard accounts of practical reasoning the agent derives an intention or proceeds to action on the basis of a desire for some goal and a belief that the action would be a means of promoting that goal. Although such sequences of reasons may involve the development of derived desires on the basis of others (I want to hang my coat up, so I desire to find the cloakroom), the picture requires that certain desires are simply brute features of our subjectivity. We will discuss this model of intentional agency in Chapter 6. Here, however, we wish to focus on the nature of desire itself.

In this chapter we explore the nature of desire by drawing a contrast between what might be termed depth and surface accounts.[4] Depth accounts see desires as inner features of agents, pushing them towards certain engagements in the world designed to satisfy the desire and thereby, in many accounts, to satisfy the person. Such desires, which we find ourselves with, may be caused by biology or by universal aspects of our psychic development, or simply by causal encounters with our world. What marks them, however, is that they can be given only causal explanations. A consequence of such a picture is that our basic desires, those which provide us with reasons for derived desires, and thereby for intentions and actions, are in a crucial respect *blind*.[5] Desires are something by which we simply find ourselves propelled. Our only role is to find ways to promote their satisfaction. A priori there seems no limit to what, on such accounts, we might find ourselves desiring (although the scientific stories might set some causal limits on this). Reflecting on such views, Anscombe remarks, 'But is not any thing wantable … ? It will be instructive to anyone who thinks this to approach someone and say, "I want a saucer of mud". He is likely to be asked what for?'[6] For Anscombe, desires have to be intelligible. If not, they are not possible, the possibility here being a constitutive not an empirical one.

The account which we would wish to endorse differs from one which offers desires as blind propulsions. As we saw in the previous chapter the world presented to us in perception has an imaginary form, which is constitutive of it. Such a form has both cognitive and affective elements. The imaginary form of our world provides us with the objects of our desires, objects which are imagined in ways which make such desiring appropriate. The imaginary has both conscious and unconscious elements, but delivers to us a world meriting desiring responses. There may be cases when we find ourselves simply assailed by desire, and it strikes us as unintelligible. But this is not the usual case. Normally we recognise that the desired object is desirable. Where this is not so we seek for special explanations, maybe in terms of the unconscious, to explain the apparent blindness and deliver to us the intelligibility of the desire.

In contrast to the picture of inner propulsions, which we simply find ourselves with, surface accounts see desires as surface modifications of the body: patterns of behaviour in relation to our environment, which have been socially imprinted. On many surface accounts the desiring behaviour which we engage in serves to constitute our identity as subjects and its inculcation is an effect of the operation of power. Initially such accounts seem better equipped to face Anscombe's question of whether it is possible to desire a saucer of mud. For many surface theorists desiring behaviour is simply the consequence of the incorporation of social norms into patterns of bodily acts. Consequently it will be possible to answer questions about the intelligibility or justification of certain desires by pointing to features of the desired object which are socially recognised as desirable. This may be its promotion of good health or smooth and unwrinkled skin. A problem with such an account, however, is that it becomes unclear why such norms should move us to act, other than as part of a causal process of conditioning. Surface accounts (deliberately) provide no account of the phenomenology of desire. In rejecting desire as an inner event propelling agents towards biologically or psychically determined ends, they also reject any account of desire which brings into play the point of view of the subject of desire, a point of view from which 'the things of the earth'[7] become desirable.

What is important about such surface accounts, nonetheless, is a recognition that desire is central to our becoming subjects: our subjectivities are desiring subjectivities. These desires not only serve to constitute us at a given point in time, but project us into future possibilities of becoming which yield a subject in process, a subject who is never finally constituted. Moreover a feature of depth accounts which we might wish to hang on to is the recognition that it is desire that keeps us moving in relation to our world, projecting us towards future possibilities. Desire then has two poles, as the quote from Butler makes clear. 'Desire is intentional in that it is always desire of or for a given object or Other, but it is also reflexive in the sense that desire is a modality in which the subject is both discovered and enhanced.'[8] In this chapter we explore these poles of desire as they negotiate the terrain between depth and surface.

Depth Accounts

Sociobiological Origins of desire

On certain, what we might term naturalistic, theories of desire, desires are conceived of as something like forces, impelling us towards our goals as a result of biological imperatives. Here a certain model prevails. Claimed universal patterns in human behaviour are noted, usually those which are shared with the animal kingdom. These universal patterns are attributed to the operation of a set of basic biological impulses conditioning our behaviour, which are required either for our survival or, in more recent sociobiological accounts, for the survival of our genes. The apparent range of objects of desire which we appear to manifest are then viewed as particular instances of these biological impulses, 'coded in the genes and moulded by natural selection'.[9] In the words of one group of commentators, everything from 'the complete system of capitalist production and distribution, to ethics and moralising ... and the alleged preference of the upper middle classes for cunnilingus and fellatio ... is explained as the product of selected genes'.[10]

There are a number of difficulties with the sociobiological programme, if it is adopted in such a wide-reaching way. The sheer variety of things which people find desirable, mediated by the specificity of historical and cultural location, makes an attempt at such widespread reduction of desire to biological promptings look highly contrived and implausible. The strategy requires a grouping together of large ranges of human and animal behaviour, as instances of universal patterns. Such a grouping requires interpretations of these human and animal behaviours as all falling under some general type, which can then be attributable to a common gene coding. It is the plausibility of such interpretations which courts controversy. Such biological accounts, moreover, appear to miss just what is distinctive about our intentional responses to the world, namely, that they are mediated by interpretive frameworks. Even acts to satisfy what might be regarded as basic needs such as hunger depend crucially on what we perceive as food, and equally what we perceive as good food or delicious food. On the sociobiological account, however, the apparent dependence of desire on our ways of interpreting and understanding the world is illusory. Such understanding may seem to provide us with objects of desire, which we can make intelligible to ourselves as desirable. In reality, however, desires operate in a *blind* way. They produce behaviour promoting certain biological ends independently of interpretive mediation. While we might *take ourselves* to be desiring, for example, to explain a framework of ideas clearly we are really engaged in promoting some biological end.

It is unclear, however, why we should accept an account which assumes that so much of our everyday explanations are misguided; and which has the consequence that our apparently intelligible seeking after desirable ends is illusory. The sociobiological picture can only be made sense of as part of a reductive strategy. This is an attempt to explain psychological characteristics in biological terms. The motivations for such reductive strategies in terms of providing scientific accounts of our dealings with the world and unifying our explanatory accounts of it have been widely discussed elsewhere. Without such motivations, however, we seem to have no reasons to reject our everyday accounts of what we find desirable in the world, in favour of one which gives as the object of desire promoting the survival of our genes, something most of us would find unintelligible.

Hydraulic Models: Russell and Freud

For many theorists writing about desire, desires are conceived of as some kind of force propelling us towards certain goals, the achievement of which leads to the cessation of the operation of the force. *What* we desire, the object of our desires, on such accounts, is the thing which will lead to the force ceasing to operate. Such a picture is found in Russell's *Analysis of Mind*.[11] We attribute desires on recognition of a certain kind of behavioural cycle, a series of actions continuing, unless interrupted, until some more or less definite state of affairs is realised. The mental state which brings about such a cycle is, for Russell, desire. It is marked by a quality of discomfort. The cycle ends (unless interrupted) when the quality of discomfort is removed. 'The state of affairs in which this condition of quiescence is achieved is called the "purpose" of the cycle.'[12] An example of such a desire for Russell is hunger, the discomfort of which is ended with the taking in of food. This then is the object of the desire. Given such a picture the articulation of the content of the desire by the agent has the possibility of going awry. The object of desire is not necessarily what we say, even to ourselves, that it is.

A model of desire with many similarities is found in the writings of Freud. Freud talks, not about desires, but about instincts or drives, which underlie all manifestations of desire. For Freud an organism works to minimise its states of excitation. Instincts are conceived of as exerting a pressure on the organism, increasing its states of tension, tension of which the organism seeks to rid itself. The release of such tension is the state of satisfaction.[13] Freud's model of the object of desire is, however, more complex than that offered by Russell. For Russell, with the paradigm of hunger in mind, the object of desire was whatever would ease discomfort, and this was more or less a factual, often biological matter, which the subject of desire could be right or wrong about. For Freud matters were not settled by biology in such a complete manner. Instincts do not dictate their own objects. Human drives are in a certain sense incomplete. They display a plasticity which is absent from Russell's account. Their objects are a consequence of the mediation of 'networks of signification and meaning'.[14] We saw, in our previous chapter, how the content of phantasy did not simply realise a preformed desire, but served to constitute its object, by its relation to the image. Such objects remain objects of a particular instinct or drive because attainment of them achieves the aim of the drive, which is the reduction of tension or excitation. Freud identifies several instincts/drives, for example: those for self preservation and sexual drives, and, later, death drives (of which more below). These drives can each take a variety of objects, dependent on individual histories and social meanings. In relation to sexual drives Elizabeth Grosz describes how the objects of these, derived from the history of subjects, and the networks of relations in which they are placed, 'retrace' purely biological instincts, whose objects are provided in the way Russell suggests. In this way an infant can gain satisfaction from sensual sucking which does not provide nourishment, and any part of the body can become ripe for sexualisation. Such a process is a consequence of what Grosz calls 'psychic takeover', an augmentation by meaning and signification provided, in the first instance, by the child's carers.[15]

On Freud's account many desires, which result from fundamental drives, are subject to repression. This is particularly the case with those desires deriving from the sexual drives. This repression is the consequence of the fundamental Oedipal drama, which, for Freud, structures the development of sexual desire. Such desire, for Freud, is constituted by the triangular relation between father, mother and child. For the boy the desire for his mother, which is the form that the sexual drive takes when it first takes an object outside of the child's own body, provokes a consequent jealousy of his father. On recognising sexual difference and recognising that his mother does not have a penis, the boy fears his love of his mother will cause castration as a punishment from his father, and the desire in this form is repressed. For the girl who also forms an initial attachment to the body of the mother, the recognition of sexual difference leads to her blaming her mother for her own perceived castration and forming an erotic attachment to the father, which also leads to conflict and repression. (There are variants on this Oedipal story to explain variations of desire along the heterosexual/homosexual axis.) This Oedipal story, for Freud, is interdependently a story about the formation of desire and a story about the formation of a subject's identity. Identity as male or female, homo or heterosexual, is constituted from the formation of desire from the sexual instincts.

When desires are repressed they are not available to consciousness and therefore the agent cannot pursue their satisfaction. The desires instead become inhibited, though they may manifest themselves in symptoms such as dreams, neuroses, etc. Unraveling neurotic symptoms requires the uncovering of such unconscious desires. In the case history of Little Hans, a child's obsessive fear of meeting horses in the street, in case they should stumble and fall down, is interpreted in terms of the horses representing, in different ways, and at different moments, both the potentially threatening father and the pregnant mother.[16]

Sexual desires, those pertaining to the satisfaction of the sexual instinct, can also, for Freud, become sublimated. Activities apparently unconnected with sexuality, for example, artistic creation and intellectual inquiry, activities with socially valued objects, are viewed by him as transformation of the sexual drives. What constitutes the psychic relation appears to be the resultant satisfaction which the new objects of desire can provide.

Despite the differences between Freud and Russell, and Freud's recognition of the mediation of basic drives by individual histories and by culture, both theorists share a model of desire in which satisfaction of desire is equated with the relief of some state of tension, resulting in an ensuing quietude. The ultimate aim of desire is the achievement of such satisfaction through the mediation of its intentional objects. In Freud's later work, however,[17] a somewhat different picture emerges. Freud places the life instincts, sexual instincts and instincts of self-preservation, in opposition to the death instincts. The death instinct displays the pattern of a search for a return to quietude, 'the fundamental tendency of every living being to return to the inorganic state ... a state of inorganic stability'.[18] Such a state, where there are no tensions and imbalances, absolute repose, is a state of annihilation. The life instincts stand, for Freud, in opposition to the death instincts. Although technically their aim is also the state of reduction of tension, they are now viewed as that which opposes such annihilation. Libido or desire, as part of the life instincts, taking either sexual objects or sublimated into some other object, are what promotes the activity of the organism, maintaining the organism in the face of the death drives. We will return to this aspect of Freud's thought later in the chapter.

Lacan and Desire as Lack

The psychoanalytic writer Lacan opposed the model of desire which Freud had offered. He refused to reduce desire to the relief of physical tension and avoids Freud's hydraulic model of psychological functioning. He makes a distinction between biological needs, which require real objects for their satisfaction, if a creature is to survive, and the domain of demand and desire which mark human engagements with the world and each other. Nonetheless Lacan's account continues to be haunted by a link between desire and satisfaction, just because for him the fulfilment of explicit demands can never provide satisfaction. Lacan's account therefore straddles the divide between depth and surface.

Following Hegel, Lacan conceives of desire as 'a fundamental lack in being', an incompleteness, which 'the subject experiences as a disquieting loss, and which prompt its activity of seeking an appropriate object to fill the lack, thus to satisfy itself'.[19] The experience of lack, for Lacan, originates in the loss of the child's relationship with the body of the mother. Such a loss is inevitable, if the child is to become an independent subject. It prompts demands which fix on objects, which can never return the child to this state of plenitude and therefore remain necessarily unsatisfactory. Demand and desire result from the entry of the subject into language. The child makes demands of the mother and later of others, for things which they are able to articulate, given the linguistic system into which they have been initiated. What forms the intentional objects of demands is then fixed by the social order into which the child is initiated, and the kinds of things which are representable linguistically, in this order, as appropriate things to want (see below for the link between this and other surface accounts). The fulfilment of these demands, however, does not yield satisfaction. For what the child actually wants is the impossible plenitude of union with another, which is impossible once they have become subjects. Consequently the apparent intentional objects of desire are merely its vehicles. The apparent satisfaction of the intentional objects of demands leaves a residual desire (for Lacan unconscious) for the imagined but impossible union with the other, which can never be satisfied. The lack of satisfaction of the imaginary desire then prompts another series of demands. The sense of lack fuels the desiring process. In the words of Bruce Fink

> Desire, strictly speaking has no object. In its essence, desire is a constant search for something else, and there is no specifiable object that is capable of satisfying it, in other words extinguishing it. Desire is fundamentally caught up in the movement of one signifier to the next, and is diametrically opposed to fixation ... It wishes merely to go on desiring.[20]

For Lacan, identity exists only in the intersubjectivity of language, the realm of the Symbolic. As we discussed in the previous chapter, this is where we bring ourselves into existence as subjects through identifying ourselves with the meanings of language which pre-exist us, and will continue to define the world after we have gone. Crucially the formation of subjects is interdependently the formation of a desire of which the phallus is the signifier. Subjects are positioned as masculine in so far as they enter into the Symbolic as those who 'have' the phallus. This position as inheritor of the phallus is confirmed by a relation to a femininity, positioned as lacking just that which masculinity has. To position oneself in language as female is to gain subjectivity only via making oneself that which is desired by men, which confirms their having the phallus. (Lacan confusingly calls this female position 'being' the phallus.) In the words of Elizabeth Grosz,

[The phallus] is the 'signifier of desire', the 'object' to which the other's desire is directed: it is insofar as he *has* the phallus that man is the object of woman's desire; and in so far as she *is* the phallus that a woman is the object of man's desire.[21]

For Lacan these are the interdependent possibilities for desire and identification offered by a Symbolic order which we necessarily adopt if we wish to become rational and autonomous subjects and agents, capable of thought and intentional agency within our world. Our subjectivity is, however, underpinned by an imaginary realm in which the phallus becomes idealised with emotional investments derived from the dream of plenitude. Such a phallus men never have and women never are. Thus the socially sanctioned patterns of give and take which we learn constitute relations of love will always fail to satisfy, for they are underpinned by desires for an imagined but impossible plenitude or fullness which we have necessarily forfeited in the course of becoming subjects.

Satisfaction and Desire

The objects of my desire are fixed by what would satisfy them. That seems like a tautology. What is far from tautological, however, is the link between what would satisfy my desires and satisfaction in the much more robust sense in which the authors we have been discussing use the term. Within models of desire anchored in such notions of satisfaction a gap opens between what we might take to be desirable and the underlying origin of our desiring activities, a gap between intentional object and cause, in which the cause is given priority and the intentional object prone to misrecognition of it. For Russell satisfaction comes with a state of quietude, yet what would produce this is often not what we take ourselves to find desirable. For Freud satisfaction comes with a reduction in the levels of tension. Our desires are manifestations of libidinal or destructive drives of which our particular goals are merely instances. Alternatively these drives get sublimated into objects, which strike us as attractive in themselves, yet turn out to be a replaying of the Oedipal drama. For Lacan satisfaction, although unachievable, is a state of fullness or plenitude. Our desiring activities originate in the sense of lack which the absence of such plenitude evokes. Within a model which sees the aim of desire as satisfaction, and also sees satisfaction as a state of plenitude which generates no further demands, it is clear why, to maintain subjectivity, our objects of demand must be permanently mismatched with what would provide such satisfaction. The alternative would be a loss of self, analogous to the kind of annihilation Freud envisages with the death drives.

What might lead us to adopt these stories of origins? Why should we think that all desires are manifestations of a few fundamental drives, the nature of which are continually misrecognised? Or that desire is fuelled by some primary sense of lack? There are occasions when we might seek an alternative explanation of behaviour than that provided by the object of desire which an agent might sincerely avow. There are times when our responses to a situation have a character which we cannot make intelligible, to ourselves or others, in terms of what strikes us as desirable/undesirable about it. A child responds with what appears like disproportionate rage to a meal which they don't particularly like. An argument between friends or partners gains an intensity which does not match the significance which either attaches to its occasion. Sometimes the lack of intelligibility only strikes us when we see a pattern of responsiveness over a period of time. Someone might fail to take opportunities to promote avowed goals for reasons, which, over time, seem trivial. On some occasions, as in cases cited by Freud, there are cycles of repetitious behaviour for which the agent is at a loss to provide any characteristics of desirability at all. There are also cases where the manner in which the agent relates to a situation belies their account of what it is that they desire. In these kinds of cases we may seek alternative objects or characteristics of desirability in the light of which the responses do become intelligible. The apparently lost opportunity can come to be seen as a protection against the threat of exposures of weakness, or as the manifestation of self-destructive impulses which will continue to operate, until they are recognised and addressed in some other way. In each of these situations the search for an alternative to the apparent object of desire has come about for specific reasons, namely, the lack of an intelligible fit between the agents' avowed desires and their responses to their situations. These are, however, specific kinds of situations. It does not seem possible to conclude from them that *all* our desires are underpinned by more basic desires, which provide the aspects under which things are really desirable, and are the moving force in producing responses to promote their satisfaction. In many/most of our everyday interactions with our environment what we take to be desirable/undesirable and what we direct our responses towards form an intelligible whole. If we break the link between desire and robust satisfaction, then we also lose the motivation for regarding the objects of desire as quite separate from its cause. Without such origin stories we can recognise that our desires for particular objects, or others, are provoked by the characteristics of these very (imaginary) objects.

There are, however, important insights from these psychoanalytic stories that we need to recognise. When Freud developed his theory of the drives he was using a hydraulic model of the mind, which we no longer find persuasive. Nonetheless he provides us with a picture of desire as that which yields a subject actively engaging with her world. Desire is that which keeps us going, prevents stasis and death. Similarly, in Lacan, the insistence on the process of desiring, rather than the objects desired, reminds us that desiring engagements are the way in which subjects are made. Both theorists tell stories about the way in which desires are structured and subjects thereby formed, the universal applicability of which we might question. In offering us the Oedipal drama Freud stresses the precariousness of its resolution. What is, nonetheless, offered is an account of the formation of subjectivity via the formation of an imaginary body and world, negotiated through affective relations with others and the mediation of culture. It is from such an imaginary world that our desires find their objects. For Lacan the structuring of the Symbolic yields a subjectivity in which desire is formed in relation to the phallus, and a position of desiring subject is problematically unavailable to those who enter the Symbolic as women. The universal necessity of such structuring has been widely challenged. Nonetheless the role of the Symbolic in mediating the possibilities for desire has formed the basis of the surface accounts we will discuss below.

Surface Accounts

What we term surface accounts of our psychic life, including our desires, reject the source or origin of desire in either a biological or psychic interiority. Indeed Foucault, one of the originators of such approaches, refuses to use the concept of desire, as he regarded it as too closely linked with naturalistic or psychoanalytic stories of origin. Instead of the source of desire being found in such interiority, surface writers explore how the apparent effect of interiority, depth, is created, on the surface of the body. For Elizabeth Grosz this project is part of a paradigm 'which conceives of subjectivity in terms of the primacy of corporeality ... on the model, not of latency or depth, but of surface'.[22] Judith Butler claims that the idea of an inner essence is a fabricated one: 'That very interiority is an effect and function of a decidedly public and social discourse ... words, acts and gestures, articulated and enacted desires create the illusion of an interior and organising ... core'.[23] Surface accounts in rejecting interiority foreground the role of social construction in the formation of desire. Here, the claims are not simply that desires are *caused* by immersion in social and cultural forms. It is rather that what gets to count as desire and enactment of desire is *constituted out* of the discourses and practices which surround a subject and in which a subject takes part. Our concepts of desire and subjectivity are 'remapped' (Grosz) in terms of corporeality. That corporeality is not a bodiliness capturable in terms of physics, but one which itself requires social practices for its articulation. Subjects are formed by processes of subjectification to social norms, which become incorporated onto their bodies. They do not precede the acts which serve to constitute them as the kind of subjects that they are. As for Lacan, the discourses at the centre of such accounts do not stand in a representational relation to desire and subjectivity, but serve to constitute them. However, for Lacan, such an account of the productivity of language, and the social norms which it embodies, is in contrast to an originary desire which we can never satisfy. He, therefore, bases his surface account upon a depth one. For theorists such as Foucault and Butler, however, the productivity of language, law and other social norms does not require the postulation of such an originary desire. All the work of depth can be done on the surface.

Foucault and the Truth about Sex

For Foucault the nineteenth century was marked by the development of a *scientia sexualis*. Here, primarily within a medical framework, an attempt was made to discover the 'truth about sex'.[24] Such a science proceeded by a clinical codification of sexual practices. Such a classification built on a tradition of confession from previous centuries, in which confessions were now replaced by clinical examinations in which medical examination, questionnaires, recollected memories and free associations were all used as methods to uncover the supposed varieties of sexual practices and reveal the basic workings of sexual desire as a deep and constitutive feature of human nature itself. This deep and constitutive character of sexual desire itself was considered not to be immediately apparent and to require the investigations of scientists to reveal its essence. The consequence of such a science being conducted within a medical framework was the development of frameworks of normal and pathological desire. Pathological desires then required medical intervention to be normalised.

For Foucault, however, there is no 'truth about sex', deeply buried requiring the excavations of scientists to uncover. The scientific investigations about sexuality were producing discourses about sexuality which were themselves productive of the very features of subjectivity which they purported to uncover.[25] These scientific discourses circulated with a number of other discourses about sex which were prevalent throughout the Victorian period. Foucault rejects the view that the Victorian period was marked by a repression of sexuality. For this to be true we would need to conceive of sexuality as a given set of desires whose manifestation was prohibited more or less effectively. For Foucault, however, the Victorian era was an era in which discourses about sex proliferated, albeit many of them took the form of prohibitions. In prohibiting something we do nonetheless have to speak about it, creating a discourse that is in circulation. The circulating discourse about sex normalised reproductive heterosexuality. Unproductive female bodies were regarded as liable to lapse into hysterical symptoms, children's masturbation as unnatural and 'perverse', non-reproductive sexual practices as a sign of pathology needing treatment. For Foucault the circulating discourses of desire were tied up with the operation of power. In the nineteenth century the discourses which he discusses were instrumental in reinforcing a norm of reproductive sex controlled by the authority of medical practitioners as well as lawyers and priests.

These circulating discourses of sexuality were, for Foucault, *productive and constitutive* of the desire which they were officially regulating. The desire, which they produced, consisted simply in the circulation of such discourses and the bodily conformity or resistance to the norms they manifest. In a parallel way to Lacan, desire, and thereby subjectivity, was only produced by subjectification to prevailing discourse, in the light of which subjects conducted their practices. Whether in accordance with privileged or prohibited forms of desire (Foucault does not address the question of the formation of some subjects in accordance with certain discourses and others with others), the circulating discourse came to constitute desire itself. On this picture subjects do not have homosexual or heterosexual desires which they learn to label. Rather, subjects come to position themselves within a discourse as heterosexual or homosexual and consequently engage in certain desiring practices. The picture is not that the norms or prohibitions are internalised to yield desire as features of an inner psychic economy. Rather they are incorporated, mapped onto a body whose practices are mou lded to cohere with them. In such a picture Foucault departs from Lacan not only in doing away with originary desire, but with regard to the nature of the Symbolic order. For Foucault there are multiple discourses in circulation at any time and they are fluid and prone to change. Pathologised desires can become normalised in the creation of reverse discourse. Our desires and identities therefore do not remain fixed but can change over time and throughout different moments of history and culture.

Butler and the Performativity of Desire

Foucault's ideas became further developed by Judith Butler.[26] Butler, like Foucault, sees social discourses and practices as productive of desiring subjects, whose desires are consequent on the kind of subjects they are positioned as. In forming ourselves, and being formed by others into, for example, girls and boys, we perform our identities according to a script provided by social norms. Such scripts dictate what kind of activities and objects are desirable, kicking footballs, playing with dolls, combing the hair of Little Ponies, playing on Gameboys etc. The notion of a performance can suggest a picture of an actor on a stage, but Butler's notion is different in crucial ways from this. First, there is no contrast between the performance and the real. The performance constitutes the real. Secondly, talking of performance can suggest a subject who is formed prior to acts and chooses which acts to perform. But for Butler, as for Foucault, there is no doer behind the deed. There are only deeds, and the subject and their desires and pleasures become constituted out of such doings (for a further discussion of performativity see Chapter 6).

Desire then, for Butler, is not something prior moving us to act and form our identities. It is not the case that prior to encountering Little Ponies our daughters had some desire seeking satisfaction, which combing and plaiting manes and tails served to satisfy. (We might be reminded here of Freud's suggestion that women's desire to plait originated in a desire for a penis and the plaiting of their pubic hair to look like a penis.) For Butler, in contrast, engaging in this way with such toys is one of the practices whereby subjects come to constitute themselves as girls. Butler gives a parallel account of bodily pleasures, which appear to have their origin in the sensitivity of particular parts of the body. She criticises 'the conflation of desire with the real – that is the belief that it is parts of the body, the "literal" penis, the "literal" vagina. which cause pleasure and desire'.[27] The body is not the 'ground or cause' of desire but rather its 'occasion or object'.[28]

> Pleasures are said to reside in the penis, the vagina and the breasts, or to emanate from them, but such descriptions correspond to a body which has already been constructed or naturalised as gender specific. In other words, some parts of the body become conceivable foci of pleasure precisely because they correspond to a normative ideal of a gender specific body. Pleasures are in some sense determined by the structure of gender whereby some organs are deadened to pleasure and others brought to life. Which pleasures shall live and which shall die is often a matter of which serve the legitimating practices of identity formation that take pace within the matrix of gender norms.[29]

Our desires and pleasures are constituted out of the moulding of our bodies to social norms. Butler also recognises that in the formation of social norms there is always an implied outside or forbidden to the norm which has to be thought, articulated if the norm is to be grasped. Consequently, it is always possible for subjects to form themselves and their desires from what is socially prohibited, to perform homosexuality instead of heterosexuality.

Butler, however, distinguishes her account from that of Foucault. She argues that a discursive account of homosexual desire, for example, can 'make the mistake of substituting the name for what it names'.[30] Here, in making such a distinction, Butler is not suggesting a return to a picture in which desire is a fixed and prior referent, which we simply have to name. There is, however, a recognition that there is something in *excess* of any given performances or discourses which leaves open the possibility of alternatives.

> Though the referent cannot be fully named, it must be kept separate from what is nameable, if only to guarantee that no name claims finally to exhaust the meaning of what we are and what we do, an event that would foreclose the possibility of becoming more and different than what we have already become.[31]

Butler's position here seems to be something like the following. It is not that there is a truth about desire, sexual or otherwise, which we represent in language and try to satisfy with practices. Nonetheless our performances, linguistic and otherwise, are not *all there is*. Desire is excessive. The possibilities of desire outrun any given performances of it. Such possibilities rule out two things. One is that desire is a determinate kind and we presently have a complete and accurate representation of it. Another is that desires are, by definition, whatever we presently count as desires. For Butler this forms the basis for her talk of an excess, something which our practices fail to exhaust, something which is open to discursive construction in alternate ways.

These accounts do away with the necessity of stories of origin by pointing to the possibilities opened up by performative play. They also foreground the link between the formation of subjectivity and the constitution of desires. For to be a subject is to be a desiring subject, and that is one who engages in certain kinds of way with the world around them. It is less clear, however, that a purely performative account of such engagement gives us a satisfactory account of the subjectivity whose formation is being theorised. Explicitly within surface theories an account of subjectivity in terms of the point of view of a subject on to the world is rejected, and replaced by an account of subjectivity as something close to a corporeal style within the world. Foucault and Butler are explicitly thinking about the self in terms of constituting practices, rather than in terms of a subject experiencing a world, which provides grounds for such practices. What is missing from these surface stories is a sense that the process of social initiation is a process of recognition, whereby subjects can come to view states of affairs as desirable, a recognition which makes sense of their ensuing activities. (See Chapter 6 for further discussion of this point.) These accounts provide for our daughters' appropriative behaviour towards their Little Ponies, without providing for the ponies' allure, a matter on which there might be some disagreement and debate. To insist on desire as a feature of a subjective point of view, as having in this way a pheno-menology, is not to retreat to the kind of psychic interiority which marked depth accounts. It is not to seek pre-given desires to ground our engagements with the world. For it is quite compatible with accepting the role which imitative performances might play in the formation of such a point of view. However, what we are being initiated into is a certain way of looking at the world. It is towards the world that the attention of the agent is directed, to find it attractive or otherwise. In the terms of our previous chapters, performative play yields an imaginary form for the agent's world, a form within which certain possibilities stand out as desirable.

Deleuze: Becoming Horse

The move away from subjectivity, which was explicitly part of Foucault's project, is carried further in the work of Deleuze. In the work of Deleuze, as it has been appropriated by recent writers, 'desire is understood, not as an individual possession but rather as a relational force among individuals'.[32] For Deleuze desire is that which makes connections between things, the lines of force which bring them together, or apart, in movements of *becoming* other than they are.

The Deleuzian picture, at which we are taking only a very selective look here, stands in opposition to many of the strands of thought which we have so far considered. Desiring encounters between entities emerge from particular encounters between individual bodies. In opposition to naturalising accounts of desire they do not result from general charac-teristics of those bodies which can be captured as laws. Moreover they cannot each be viewed as a playing out of the Oedipal drama which marked the Freudian accounts. In discussing Freud's treatment of the case of Little Hans, Deleuze argues that it is reductive and abusive to interpret Little Hans's story as simply a variant of the mother/father/child triad. The boy wanders the streets, his desire to see the little rich girl taking him past the horses' stable. Deleuze comments, 'Bizarrely the wish to explore the building strikes Freud as the desire to sleep with the mother', and later he remarks,

> As if the 'vision' of the street, frequent at the time – a horse falls, is beaten, struggles – wasn't capable of directly affecting the libido, and has to recall his parents having sex ... the identification of the horse with the father touches on the grotesque.[33]

In contrast to accounts of desire which foreground lack and satisfaction, Deleuze sees desire as a positive and productive force, not originating in lack. It does not have a goal which simply serves as its endpoint or terminus. Desiring encounters are ongoing and do not yield single endpoints.

In contrast to other surface accounts, however, desire is not seen as a consequence of processes of normalisation. Rather, 'every position of desire, no matter how small, is capable of calling into question the established order of society; not that desire is asocial, on the contrary. But it is explosive.'[34] For Deleuze, desire is 'machinic'. It makes connections between entities. In recent appropriations, in the work, for example, of Elspeth Probyn and Elizabeth Grosz, Deleuze's conception of desiring encounters as processes of bodily becoming has been foregrounded. For Elizabeth Grosz, 'Desire ... experiments, producing ever new ... linkages, and connections ... meandering, creative, non-repetitive, proliferative, unpredictable'.[35] For Elspeth Probyn, Deleuze highlights the singularity and specificity of desire; the immediacy of encounters which keep us moving forward and becoming other than we are. Such movements are an effect of our proximity to other bodies, which, in Deleuze's words, casts shadows on to us. In discussing Deleuze's treatment of the story of Little Hans, Probyn clarifies how this process of becoming is a bodily one and requires a transformation of our image of our bodies.

> It is not that the little boy transposes the horse ... onto the father, nor is it that the horse has some mythical standing; rather, in a common way Little Hans becomes-horse ... Becoming-horse thus designates a moment of valency and microcombination between the image the boy has of his body in relation to the horse. This in between moment ... entails a certain dissolution of the body image as known, as *my* body, in favour of another image, that of becoming horse.[36]

Probyn highlights a similar moment in the film *National Velvet*.

> The desire to become-horse is unmistakable in scenes that show Liz, [the young Liz Taylor], in her bed repeating and being caught up in the motion of riding,

her arms stretched forward, her legs straining ... these shots catch the lines of flight between girl and horse and dwell on the inbetween-ness of two machinic entities.[37]

Judith Butler, in her early work, criticises Deleuze's model of desire. She sees him as putting forward an emancipatory model based on 'the reification of mutiplicitous affect as the invariant, though largely repressed, ontological structure of desire ... The postulation of a natural multiplicity appears, then, an insupportable metaphysical speculation'.[38] For Butler, this 'appeal to a precultural eros ignores the Lacanian insight that all desire is linguistically and culturally constructed'.[39] It is the location of desire in social and historical terms which she sees as necessary to avoid such unacceptable ontologies. There appears some force to Butler's criticisms given Deleuze's own descriptions of the emancipatory potential of desire to break down the normalising structures of society. Desire for Deleuze is, however, non-substantial, and exists not as a pre-given force pushing us towards encounters with others (as in depth accounts), but as *relations* between specific bodies which arise in particular social and material milieus. The specificity and unpredictability of desiring encounters to which he points helps rescue us from 'too exclusive an understanding of our psychic life as the effect of normalisation'.[40] Butler's recognition of the excessiveness of desire addresses similar concerns. We suggest here that we understand desire, on this account, as an ongoing process of desiring encounters, not as a metaphysical force lying behind encounters and driving them.

More problematic, however, is the radical depersonalisation of Deleuze's account. In common with other surface theorists Deleuze does not accept a preformed subject, with sets of desires who then chooses which encounters to engage in. Subjects are formed out of desiring encounters and are open to ongoing processes of becoming other. However, these processes, which result in the formation of subjects, are not different in kind from those which constitute rocks or plants. What has become quite lost is a view of subjects as those with points of view onto a world which matters to them, and with its loss goes the phenomenology of desire. Probyn highlights the way 'desire touches off and sets in motion different possibilities, a movement of attraction that Foucault sees in "a woman's gesture in a window", a door left ajar, the smile of a guard before a forbidden threshold'.[41] But what makes this the workings of desire, not magnetism, for example, is someone who sees the attraction in the woman's gesture, and anticipates the pleasures behind the door. Insisting on the reinstitution of such subjectivity is not necessarily to reinstate a subject who is formed independently of desiring encounters, or one with the coherence and continuity which surface writers have been at pains to reject. It certainly is not to require a transcendent subject with authority over its own psychic life. It is, however, to mark a difference between the kinds of configurations which result from engagements of micro-particulars. Some are subjects who find themselves in a world where the shadows of other bodies not only produce effects, but are perceptible in ways that make those effects intelligible to their subjects. Deleuze then shares a problem with other surface theorists. In refusing psychic depth, the allure of the desired object and the subject's recognition of it gets lost.

Existential and Phenomenological Accounts of Desire

In Carolyn Steedman's biography of her mother she characterises her mother's life as marked by longing. The longing here was for real material things: 'However that longing was produced in her distant childhood, what she actually wanted were real things, real entities which she materially lacked, things that a culture and a social system withheld from her.'[42] Such things had a concrete materiality interwoven with an imaginary salience. They promised glamour. Moreover they signalled to her a way 'to be what she wasn't'. The longing for those real things was reflexive. It was a longing for new possibilities for herself.

When we turn to existential and phenomenological accounts of desire we find desire becomes a mode in which such a subject's world is apprehended. The assumption of such subjectivity does not make desires something which we look inwards to detect. Desires, as Sartre insists, are not 'contained' in consciousness.

> The empirical psychologist ... views desire as being 'in' man by virtue of being 'contained' by his consciousness, and he believes that the meaning (content) of the desire is inherent in the desire itself ... But if I desire a house or a glass of water or a woman's body, how could this body, this glass, this piece of property reside in my desire ... how can my desire be any thing but the consciousness of these objects as desirable? Let us beware then of considering these desires as little psychic entities dwelling in consciousness; they are consciousness itself in its original projective structure.[43]

In a parallel way Sartre rejects accounts of desire based on instinct, satisfaction, or the pursuit of pleasure and cessation of pain. Desire is not something whose goal is its own cessation. ('We desire a particular woman, and not simply our sexual satisfaction.')[44]

Heidegger (rather more obscurely) makes a similar point.

> But affectedness is very remote from anything like coming across a psychical condition by the kind of apprehending which first turns around and then back.

Indeed it is so far from this that only because 'there' has already been disclosed in affectedness can immanent reflection come across 'experiences' at all.[45]

The possibility of introspectively discovering that we are experiencing desire rests on something outside ourselves previously being disclosed to us as desirable. Both Sartre and Heidegger allow for our desires to have a certain kind of intelligibility to us. Sartre criticises psychological accounts, which 'refer us ultimately to inexplicable original givens'.[46] The desires which we simply find ourselves with on such an assumption would not be meaningful or intelligible to us. But our desires *do* make sense to us, in virtue of the desirability we detect in their objects. In this framework the way in which we perceive objects carries with it an affective quality.

There are nonetheless important differences in the accounts offered by Sartre and Heidegger regarding the 'affective intentionality' which is constitutive of desire. For Sartre's account requires a 'for itself', a transcendent subject whose choices are, in some sense, the source of value in the world. Referring to the experience of the alarm clock ringing and summoning us to work he insists, 'it is I who confer on the alarm clock its exigency – I and I alone',[47] and again, 'it is I who sustain values in being. I make my decision concerning them – without justification and without excuse'.[48] The picture Sartre is offering here is not, however, the projective one which we find in philosophers such as Hume. For Hume, values exist in the world as a result of our projecting our subjective feelings on to it. A state of affairs strikes me as desirable because I have a prior desire which such a state of affairs will be a means of satisfying. For Sartre there are no such prior desires to be found within our breast (and if there were they would be unintelligible to us). For Heidegger subjects find themselves thrown into a world which is already significant and salient to them. There is no suggestion that they themselves are responsible for the affective quality of the world, although it is something on which they can reflect and consequently modify their response. Subjectivity is constituted out of the way in which the world appears to those in the midst of it. We do not have, as in Sartre, a transcendent subject who is the source of the value in the world. Rather 'existentially, affectedness implies a disclosive submission to the world, out of which we can encounter something that matters to us'.[49]

Nonetheless, in attending to the phenomenology of desire in both writers, the contrast between them becomes less stark. Sartre characterises desire as the ensnarement of our bodies by the world in the midst of which we find ourselves.

> In my desiring perception, I discover something like a *flesh* of objects. My shirt rubs against my skin, and I feel it ... the warmth of air, the breath of the wind, the rays of sunshine etc., all are present to me in a certain way ... revealing my flesh by means of their flesh ...The world is made ensnaring.[50]

In this discussion Sartre highlights the bodiliness of these desiring encounters which was given priority in the work of both Butler and Deleuze: 'consciousness is engulfed in a body which is engulfed in a world'.[51] Later Sartre discusses our finding certain objects 'slimy'. The sliminess is not encountered as a brute feature of the world independent of us. But neither is it simply the projection of some feeling from within us onto the world. From the start the object is 'charged with an affective meaning'.[52]

> [T]he slimy appears as already the outline of a fusion of the world with myself ... what comes back to us ... as an objective quality is a new nature which is neither material (and physical) nor psychic, but which transcends the opposition of the psychic and the physical.[53]

Here Sartre seems to be characterising the affective qualities of the world as perspectival qualities, features which require the perspective of engaged subjects to be made visible. This picture seems in principle detachable from his insistence on a transcendent subject whose choices are the source of the values she consequently perceives. In the terminology of the previous chapter, what the phenomenological account of desire offers us is desire as a mode of apprehending an imaginary world (in which, for Steedman's mother, fine clothes are tinged with glamour).

Desire has two poles; the objects desired and the desiring subjects. The ensnaring qualities of the world constitutively open up possibilities of becoming for the subjects who apprehend them. Following Hegel, and consequently with echoes of Lacan, Sartre views desire as a manifestation of *lack* or absence or negation at the heart of being. By experiencing desire subjects grasp themselves as incomplete beings, reaching out for another state.

> All desire ... be it for a woman, for the world, or for God, has a similar structure, root and meaning. All desire ... refers back to the totality of the subject's *élans vers l'etre* ... his *impulse towards being* – back to his original relation to himself, to the world and to the other.

Desire, for Sartre, brings the subject into being, by beginning the process of creating itself through acts: 'desire is the being of human reality'.[54] It also reveals to a subject its corporeality: 'Objects become the transcendent ensemble which reveals my incarnation to me. A contact with them is a caress ... to perceive an object when I am in the desiring attitude is to caress myself with it.'[55]

As Sartre develops his phenomenology of desire, however, it becomes clear that for him desire necessarily fails. Initially, it appears we can desire to possess an object, to be someone or to do something.[56] In fact, he concludes, these are all forms of the desire for possession. If I possess an object, however, it becomes consumed/appropriated by me and thereby loses its identity. Or it remains separate and unaffected by my desire, so my desire fails (the consequence of this model in relation to the desire for an other will be explored in Chapter 7). Sartre then ultimately offers us a picture of desire, which, like Lacan's, is doomed to failure. It is not clear, however, why we should accept an attempt to reduce desire to a form of appropriative possession. Heidegger also recognises a reflexivity inherent in our affective relations to the world. In finding things desirable we are envisaging certain possibilities for *ourselves* in relation to them. Velvet in imagining the horse is imagining possibilities of herself in relation to the horse. Steedman's mother imagined possibilities for herself, transformed by fine clothes and luxurious surroundings. It seems undermotivated to characterise these possibilities in terms of appropriative incorporation and thereby to conclude that desire is ultimately self defeating. But the fundamental insight, that desire is constitutive of self, remains.

Summary

We would like to suggest that an account of desire does not need to rest on depth accounts anchored in biological processes or fundamental drives. Instead we can view desire as our own imagined becomings in relation to an imagined world. Such a view borrows from phenomenological accounts a recognition that desire is a mode of experiencing the world as desirable, a mode in which the imagined shape of the interdependent world and self is revealed by our responsiveness to it. It borrows from surface accounts the awareness that such imagined shapes are discursively constituted. This picture allows that our desires should be intelligible to ourselves and others, and not promptings which we simply stumble across in our inner streams of consciousness. The imaginary shape, which our world takes, reflects both personal histories and cultural initiation. It can, however, have an unpredictability and singularity which outruns both. Judith Butler, while recognising the operation of power in the social constitution of desirability, nonetheless signals an excessiveness to desire which outruns it. For Deleuze desiring encounters reflect the singularity and contingency of bodies encountering each other, in ways not susceptible to general-isation.

Many of the accounts we have discussed share the insight that desire constitutes the subject in process. Freud's opposition of the life instincts to the death instincts; the insistence on desiring as a process in Lacan; Sartre's impulse towards being; and the forward movement of change and becoming which we have distilled from Deleuze; each tries to capture desire as that which yields a subject in the process of becoming. This process prevents fixity and determination, and yields a temporal dimension to subjectivity.

Notes

1. C. Steedman, *Landscape for a Good Woman* (London: Virago, 1986), p. 6.
2. J. Lacan, Seminar XIII, 'L'objet de la psychanalyse', 1965–6, unpublished, quoted in B. Fink, *The Lacanian Subject* (Princeton: Princeton University Press, 1995), p. 90.
3. J. Butler, *Subjects of Desire* (New York: Columbia University Press, 1987), p. 25.
4. For the contrast between depth and surface accounts of mentality see E. Grosz, *Volatile Bodies* (Bloomington and Indianapolis: Indiana University Press, 1994).
5. The description of such desires as blind derives from P. Gilbert, *Human Relationships* (Oxford: Blackwell, 1991), p. 28.
6. G. E. M. Anscombe, *Intention* (Oxford: Blackwell, 1957), p. 70.
7. Steedman, *Landscape for a Good Woman*, p. 7.
8. Butler, *Subjects of Desire*, p. 25.
9. R. Lewontin, S. Rose and L. Kamin, *Not in Our Genes: Biology, Ideology and Human Nature* (London and New York: Penguin, 1984), p. 275.
10. Ibid., p. 238.
11. B. Russell, *Analysis of Mind* (London: Allen and Unwin, 1921).
12. Ibid., p. 75.
13. See S. Freud, 'Three Essays on the Theory of Sexuality', in S. Freud, *The Standard Edition of the Complete Psychological Works of Sigmund Freud*, trans. J. Strachey (London: Hogarth Press, 1953–73), vol. VII, and 'Instincts and Their Vicissitudes', in ibid., vol. XIV.
14. E. Grosz, *Volatile Bodies*, p. 56.
15. Ibid.
16. S. Freud, 'Analysis of a Phobia in a Five Year Old Boy', in Freud, *Standard Edition*, vol. X.
17. S. Freud, 'Beyond the Pleasure Principle', in Freud, *Standard Edition*, vol. XVIII.
18. J. Laplanche and J. B. Pontalis, *The Language of Psychoanalysis* (London: Karnac, 1973), p. 102.
19. E. Grosz, *Sexual Subversions: Three French Feminists* (Sydney: Allen and Unwin, 1989), p. xvi.
20. Fink, *Lacanian Subject*, pp. 90–1.
21. Grosz, *Sexual Subversions*, p. xx.
22. Grosz, *Volatile Bodies*, p. viii.
23. J. Butler, *Gender Trouble* (New York and London: Routledge, 1990), p. 71.

24. M. Foucault, *The History of Sexuality*, vol. 1, trans. R. Hurley (London: Allen and Unwin, 1978).
25. Ibid., p. 11.
26. Butler, *Gender Trouble*.
27. Ibid., p. 71.
28. Ibid.
29. Ibid., p. 70.
30. J. Butler, *Excitable Speech* (New York: London Routledge, 1997), p. 125.
31. Ibid.
32. E. Probyn, *Outside Belongings* (New York and London: Routlege, 1996), p. 25.
33. G. Deleuze, quoted in Probyn, *Outside Belongings*, p. 50.
34. G. Deleuze and F. Guattari, *Anti-Oedipus: Capitalism and Schizophrenia*, trans. R. Hurley, M. Seem and H. Lane (Minneapolis: University of Minneapolis Press, 1983), p. 116.
35. Grosz, *Volatile Bodies*, p. 163.
36. Probyn, *Outside Belongings*, p. 51.
37. Ibid., p. 54.
38. Butler, *Subjects of Desire*, p. 214.
39. Ibid.
40. B. Martin, 'Sexualities without Genders and Other Queer Utopias', *diacritics*, 24, 1994, pp. 104–21, p. 106.
41. Probyn, *Outside Belongings*, p. 13.
42. Steedman, *Landscape for a Good Woman*, p. 6.
43. J.-P. Sartre, *Being and Nothingness*, trans. Hazel Barnes (London: Routledge, 1995), p. 557.
44. Ibid., p. 384.
45. M. Heidegger, *Being and Time*, trans. J. Macquarrie (Oxford: Blackwell, 1962), H 136.
46. Sartre, *Being and Nothingness*, pp. 559–60.
47. Ibid., p. 38.
48. Ibid., p. 39.
49. Heidegger, *Being and Time*, H 137.
50. Sartre, *Being and Nothingness*, p. 392.
51. Ibid.
52. Ibid., p. 604.
53. Ibid., p. 606.
54. C. Howells, 'Sartre: Desiring the Impossible', in H. Silverman (ed.), *Philosophy and Desire* (New York and London: Routledge, 2000), p. 91.
55. Sartre, *Being and Nothingness*, p. 392.
56. See discussion in Howells, 'Sartre', pp. 92–3.

5

Emotions

Affect and Cognition

By the time you have reached this point in the book you may be exasperated, excited, intrigued or merely bored. Whatever your reaction, if you have any reaction at all you will most likely be experiencing some emotion. But what are emotions, and why do we experience them? Could we be much the sort of creatures that we are, with all our other experiences, thoughts and desires, and yet be devoid of emotional feelings? And if we could not, is that because our emotions somehow derive from these other psychological states, or do they add some indispensable element to them? In particular, how do the distinctive *bodily* reactions of emotion figure in our necessary commerce with the world? Are, for example, the yawns of the bored reader or the knitted brow and grinding teeth of the exasperated one merely disturbances in her sensible business of getting on with what she has set herself to do? Or do they in some way play an essential part in her active engagement with things?

There is a compelling picture of our role as agents in the world which makes this seem impossible. It is one that views us as essentially rational creatures whose experiences of the world allow us to change it in various ways to suit the ends that satisfy our desires. The standard explanations of our actions are ones that represent them as directed to such satisfaction in accordance with our beliefs derived from our experience. In a word, such explanations *rationalise* our actions.[1] In doing so they make the actions intelligible not just as what agents in these psychological circumstances do do, but as what it is appropriate for them to do, so that the agent can identify with her actions as ones she had reasons for. It is not obvious that explanations of our actions by reference to emotions function in the same way. To say she yawned because she was bored may seem simply to report a regularity in human behaviour, as unintelligible to its subject as to anyone else; she may learn of her state only by noting her reactions, and perhaps repudiate it, battling to finish the forbidding volume.

It is cases like these, where an emotion comes over someone and leads to behaviour which apparently falls outside the range of their ordinary purposive activity, that generate the supposition of a sharp contrast between normal rational actions and aberrant emotional ones – a supposition in which the latter look dispensable and, as philosophers since at least the Stoics have claimed, better dispensed with, whether by a drastic change of lifestyle or a severe mental training. But is the contrast just? Consider a powerful evocation of emotion from Turgenev's novel *Liza*, in which Lavretsky suddenly discovers that his wife Varvara has been unfaithful from picking up a letter she has dropped:

> Several minutes passed; a half hour passed. Lavretsky still stood there, clenching the fatal note in his hand and gazing unmeaningfully on the floor. A sort of dark whirlwind seemed to sweep round him, pale faces to glimmer through it.
>
> A painful sensation of numbness had seized his heart. He felt as if he were falling, falling into a bottomless abyss.
>
> The soft rustle of a silk dress roused him from his torpor by its familiar sound. Varvara Pavlovna came in hurriedly from out of doors. Lavretsky shuddered all over and rushed out of the room. He felt that at that moment he was ready to tear her to pieces, to strangle her with his own hands, at least to beat her all but to death in peasant fashion ... he fled from the house.[2]

And Lavretsky eventually writes a letter of separation.

Certainly this case is one where the agent is overcome with emotion and either engages in actions which seem to serve no purpose – he 'still stood there ... gazing unmeaningfully on the floor' – or is inclined to engage in actions of which he thinks better – 'he was ready to tear her to pieces ... he fled from the house'. Furthermore these actions and inclinations are manifestations of bodily sensations – 'a sensation of numbness had seized his heart', 'he shuddered all over' – sensations which seem to owe little to the way the world impinges upon people and provides them with information about their environment. The reactions and sensations involved are also highly personal ones. Placed in the same situation others might react and feel differently from Lavretsky, with despair, perhaps, rather than anger, and thus with the different inclinations and sensations despair involves. In emotions, then, we seem to be passive, to be affected physically, and to be affected in a personal way: whereas in the ordinary rational states with which they supposedly contrast we are active, engaged with the world through mental deliberation, and so engaged impersonally, in the sense that others would likely adopt similar strategies in the same circumstances.

For all that, however, there are large similarities between the supposedly contrasting cases. In the first place, the emotional case is, like its supposedly uncomplicatedly rational counterpart, usually a response to happenings in the world which we experience. Emotions can come over us without any apparent occasion in the outside world, as indeed we can form strategies for action which are not a response to such changes, but typically they do not: they arise from our experience, or at least from our thoughts about the world. Secondly, our emotional reactions do reflect the character of that experience: they are, in a way that certainly needs some clarification here, geared to it, rather than being its arbitrary products. Yawning, when bored, for example, is not arbitrary in the way that yawning when sleepy is – a mere fact about the human condition. For what it reflects is precisely the *soporific* character of a boring experience, much as calmly cupping one's hands over one's ears reflects the deafeningly loud character of the experience of an explosion to which this is the rational reaction. And thirdly, just as many such rational reactions aim to change the world, rather than just our experience of it, so do many emotional ones. Lavretsky's inclination to strangle his wife would, if indulged, have effected such a change just as much as his coolly separating from her.

Theories of emotion may, then, stress the apparent contrast with supposedly ordinary cases, or, alternatively, the similarities with them. Thus, on the one hand, what we may term *affective* theories see emotions as a class of felt experiences involving bodily sensations and their concomitant physical reactions, but differing from *mere* bodily feelings in either or both their distinctive felt qualities and their causes and consequences. Thus the heartache of love differs from indigestion pains in arising from the beloved's attractions and leading to thoughts of them, rather than from overeating and to thoughts of relief, and may differ too in how it feels. This is, for example, David Hume's theory, [3] and it captures the passivity of emotion, its bodily affects and, perhaps its personal nature, if the same circumstances are allowed to affect different people differently. Yet it fails to show how emotion is *itself* a response to circumstances in the world, rather than leading to such a response by way of thoughts which, on Hume's account, give the emotion's object. And on failing to show the relation of emotion to the world it fails to show how emotional experiences are primarily experiences *of* the world and not just of the body, so that it is perceived features of the world to which we react emotionally.

It is to supply this deficiency that there arise, on the other hand, so-called *cognitive* theories of emotion, in which emotions are regarded as, in some sense, judgements about the world, in particular, judgements which evaluate the significance of happenings in the world for the subject: their threat to her in the case of fear, their charm in some cases of love and so on. It is because they embody such evaluations that emotions *move* us to act, and they do so much as, in the supposedly standard case, a combination of desire and belief does, providing our reason for acting. To the objection that our emotions can run counter to our settled judgements, that we can be afraid of spiders, say, even if we know they are harmless, it can be replied that the evaluations in question differ from reflective judgements in being ways we see the world, or construe it to be, much as we continue to see optical illusions in a certain way even when we know they are illusions. Yet, unlike such illusions, emotions are, on this theory, to a large extent susceptible to change, depending upon how rational we take their evaluations to be.

Thus on cognitive theories emotional behaviour is much closer to the supposedly standard case than on affective ones, in that it is a species of our active, deliberate engagement with the world and answerable to impersonal standards of rationality. What such theories leave out, of course, is precisely what affective ones highlight: the way emotions assail us uninvited, the bodily reactions and sensations this involves and the highly personalised character of many such responses. What is needed is an account of emotion that somehow brings out how these apparently contrasting features fit together and, especially, how the bodily character of our emotional responses is nonetheless crucially involved in the particular perspective on the world with which an emotion provides us.

The Difficulty of the World

One striking attempt to meet this demand is the account of emotion set forth in Sartre's early work, *Sketch for a Theory of the Emotions*, which is best approached by way of one of Sartre's examples – fainting away from fear. This, Sartre notes, is 'a behaviour of *escape*; the fainting away is a refuge'. 'But', he continues, 'let no one suppose that it is a refuge for me, that I am trying to save *myself* or to *see no more* of the ferocious beast.'[4] Instead, he suggests, I have annihilated the danger which I cannot escape by other means through suppressing my consciousness of it. What happens is that the subject's world is transformed through a transformation of their body, a process that Sartre likens to falling asleep and dreaming.[5] All this is, of course, something that happens pre-reflectively and that is not experienced as the deliberate act of the subject, but rather as something that comes over her. But the key point, for our present purposes, is that it is through bodily reactions and their concomitant sensations that things in the world are experienced as, under the influence of an emotion, they are, as frightening, horrible or whatever.

What are we to make of Sartre's theory? While the foregoing account of 'passive' fear may seem plausible we should note that Sartre's story is intended to be fully generalisable – it applies, for example, also to 'active' fear in which the subject runs away rather than faints. This, Sartre comments, is 'mistakenly supposed to be rational behaviour', whereas 'we do not take flight to reach shelter: we flee because we are unable to annihilate ourselves in unconsciousness. Flight is fainting away in action.'[6] Only such an account, Sartre believes, can explain the emotional character of this behaviour, which is a response to a sudden change in the way the world is perceived; for 'no emotional apprehension of an object as frightening ... can arise except against the background of a complete alteration of the world',[7] an alteration in which 'the world of the utilizable vanishes abruptly'[8] and is replaced by another to which we respond in the ways characteristic of emotional behaviour – ways that Sartre describes as 'magical', since they aim to change the world, but do not do so by utilising objects as instruments to achieve the agent's purposes. The magical behaviour resorted to in emotion is not, then, deliberately purposive.

It is as a supposedly general account of emotions that Richard Wollheim demurs at Sartre's theory, seeing it instead as plausible only for what he terms 'malformed emotion', namely, emotion arising when a person is unable to tolerate the experience of having some desire frustrated or, indeed, satisfied; and, Wollheim maintains, 'Sartre talks only about malformed emotions.'[9] It would, then, be because someone cannot tolerate their desire to escape the ferocious beast being frustrated that they faint, something which is 'an inapposite response',[10] and this contrasts with properly formed emotions in which frustration or satisfaction of desire is coped with appropriately. The transformation of the world which Sartre officially attributes to all emotions is, on Wollheim's reading, a state of 'phantasy', rather than an attitude to the world in which its actual properties are discerned. It is only as such a phantasy, which 'tends to occlude any aspect of the world that might falsify the phantasy',[11] that Wollheim finds Sartre's view that the emotional transformation of the world is total intelligible, for someone who can cope with the outcome of her desires has no motive for changing the world through phantasy, rather than acting in it as it really is.

Sartre introduces his theory of emotion by an oblique reference to Aesop's fable of the fox who, unable to reach the grapes he desires, passes them off as too green in order to overcome the 'disagreeable tension' which arises when 'the potentiality cannot be actualised'. 'If emotion is play-acting', as, Sartre suggests, play acting goes on in this example, 'then,' he comments, 'the play is one that we believe in'.[12] If emotions do indeed have the structure of this example then Wollheim's account would seem to be correct. But Sartre is not, in fact, implying this. The example is an analogy for the way emotions involve the attribution of qualities of the world not otherwise attributable, and do so through a particular type of behaviour. Yet this behaviour is not a compensation for something else – fainting for really escaping, for example – nor are the qualities ones that are not really in the world. The 'difficulty' of the world, to which Sartre sees the behaviour as a response, 'is a quality of the world given to perception', not 'a relation to oneself',[13] as Wollheim assumes. 'There is', for instance, 'horrible-ness in the world',[14] and not merely in one's phantasies. For this reason there is no sense in which emotional behaviour is 'inapposite' as Wollheim claims of Sartre's supposedly 'malformed' emotions. 'All ways are barred', Sartre stresses, and 'nevertheless we must act'.[15]

The feature of the fox and grapes fable that misleads Wollheim in his interpretation of Sartre is that it involves a *change* of attitude to the situation when it is realised that a desire is frustrated, and it is this change that Wollheim equates with the transformation of the world that Sartre discerns in all emotions. But the transformation in question is not a change in the way the same situation is regarded. Rather it is a change from our supposedly ordinary instrumental dealings in the world to the distinctively emotional – the magical – response. This may well be our *first* response to the situation we confront, to which no alternative attitude is even contemplated. It may be that Sartre himself was less than clear about this distinction, and did conflate a perfectly general account of the constitution of the world in emotions and a much more limited one of why we react to a world somehow indepen-dently recognised as instrumentally 'difficult' by magically transforming it. But if that is the case Wollheim's psychoanalytic development of the latter theory does not touch upon the former, since evidently they are quite independent. For while the former theory tells us what it is like to recognise the difficulty of the world through experiencing it emotion-ally, the latter is only about the emotions *consequent* upon a non-emotional recognition of this feature. Sartre, I suggest, was principally concerned with the former.

It is the former more general account which needs exploring, and which Wollheim neglects through overlooking the importance of bodily reactions to Sartre's theory. For Wollheim, 'the person's picture of the world is changed ... through the will, which is, in turn, a piece of thinking'.[16] Sartre does think that even our bodily reactions are, in some sense, willed, though not through thinking. Rather '*to believe* in magical behaviour one must be physically upset'.[17] It is through our physical reactions to certain situations which upset the ordinary equilibrium of our behavioural responses that the altered picture of the world presented by emotions is brought into view and provides a reason for our emotional engagement with it. This picture of the world is not, for Sartre, one which simply thinking could possible bring about. For it is not a picture in which the ordinary facts of a situation are somehow phantasisingly occluded or changed, in response to inner drives that make them uncomfortable. Rather, as Sartre repeatedly stresses, the *whole* world is changed, very much as in Wittgenstein's *Tractatus* the whole world of the happy man is said to be different from that of the unhappy man, even though the facts of their worlds are just the same.[18]

The properties of the world to which our emotional reactions alert us are not ones that could otherwise be grasped. That the ferocious beast is frightening, for example, is not graspable except through such reactions as Sartre describes. But this does not mean that it is not *really* frightening, but that this property is only projected upon it, as Wollheim's account implies. For the fact that such properties can only be apprehended on the basis of our responses to them does not imply that they are not really properties of the thing, any more than the fact that colours, say, are perceivable only by creatures able to respond differentially to them implies that things are not really coloured. The difference between the cases lies, as I have suggested earlier, in the relatively more *personal* character of the emotional response, and that, we can now see, depends upon differences in bodily reactions. The darkness of the world which Turgenev's Lavretsky experiences, for instance, is part and parcel of his numbness, his initial incapacity to find any way of acting in response to the discovery of his wife's infidelity. Yet here we can see his paralysis not just as an escape mechanism, but as revelatory of the way a world *is*, when such situations cannot be coped with coolly. And that they cannot is due, one might say, to the weakness of the flesh, to the vulnerability of the body, or at least of some bodies, to events which unsettle its normal functioning. But being so unsettled reveals the 'difficult' features of the world which have this effect, and reveals them in the particular character of this upset – its threateningness, its intractability and so forth.

It is because the body is essentially involved in these perceptions that emotions do commonly involve bodily sensations. That is to say, in the course of an emotional experience attention can switch from the world to the body and vice versa. Sartre regards this awareness of the body as a secondary kind of reflexive awareness, for usually I am aware of the features of the world which evoke an emotional response, rather than the bodily transformation in virtue of which the response to these features is possible.[19] But sometimes it is otherwise, and the character of the emotion is not recognised whereas the bodily sensations are. What Lavretsky is feeling, for example, and what it is about the world that makes him feel it, are less clear to him than that 'a painful sensation of numbness had seized his heart' and 'he felt as if he were falling'. And here the *obscurity* of his emotion is, in part, due to the fact that it is unclear what reason it gives him for action, so that his attention fixes upon how it affects him and not upon what in the world invites a response – a situation that changes as soon as his wife enters the room.

Sartre's stress on the fact that the horribleness, disquietingness and so on to which our bodily reactions alert us are 'in the world', as it is revealed through them, reverses the order of events on which Wollheim believes the emotions depend and which he discerns in Sartre's account. For Wollheim thinks that emotions form as a result of the satisfaction and frustration of pre-existing desires,[20] and malformed emotions from an inability to tolerate such satisfaction or frustration. Yet Sartre's account views the desires from which the emotional subject acts – to escape in the case of fear, say – as deriving from a perception of the frighteningness of the situation, a feature which cannot be coped with through attempting to fulfil one's ordinary pre-existing desires, like the prudent desire for shelter from danger. But how are we to understand, on what I have termed Sartre's most general account of the constitution of the world through emotional behaviour, his idea that 'the real meaning of fear' is 'a consciousness whose aim is to negate something in the world'?[21] It is that fear involves a desire whose fulfilment is the substitution (though on the general account this is not to be interpreted temporally) of one state of feeling (or absence of feeling) for another. Insofar as safety is desired in fear, for example, what is sought is a certain state of mind – a state of mind characterisable only as a recognition of the absence in the world of that which is fearful. As such, this desire presupposes emotion; it is not a desire from which emotion could derive.

This gives the form of what one might term the *negative* emotions. But in the positive ones too, like joy, there is, Sartre believes, a desire for a world different from the difficult one we encounter, a world that 'seems easy'.[22] That world is brought into being by joyful behaviour, whose genuineness, in the sense of its representing a response to a believed-in world, is again measured by the 'purely physiological phenomena' of a 'disordered body' which give rise to bodily sensations.[23] Yet in all cases of emotion it is only, Sartre claims, because our behaviour is motivated by this specific type of desire that such sensations do disclose the world's emotive features. Without it they would be mere bodily sensations, but, conversely, the desire distinctive of emotion is present only because of them. This is not to say, of course, that a desire of this sort is reflectively present to the subject. Rather, the desire is expressed in behaviour which has no explanation in terms of manipulating objects in 'the world of the utilisable' to satisfy the ordinary desires of that world.

The Pervasiveness of Moods

While Sartre is, I have claimed, primarily concerned with accounting for the way bodily reactions are crucially involved in an emotion's providing us with a particular perspective in the world, he nevertheless maintains a sharp contrast between what he sees as ordinary unemotional behaviour and occasional outbreaks of emotional activity. The former is viewed, as in the traditional picture, as rational instrumental action, the latter, as we have seen, as merely magical – a way of affecting the world that lacks any means/ends efficacy. And, although Sartre concedes that 'there is an existential structure of the world that is magical' and that 'the social world is primarily magical',[24] there is a strong sense that 'the world of the utilizable' is somehow the primary one and the magical world is aberrant, even, it has been suggested,[25] inherently an area of bad faith. Yet it is not clear that, on the general reading suggested, Sartre's theory really requires such a sharp contrast, nor, as we shall go on to see, that such a contrast is at all acceptable.

All the examples of emotion that Sartre considers in the *Sketch* have in common that the qualities they discern in the world affect what I take the world to require from me. In fainting from fear, action becomes impossible because the world 'is too horrible to confront"; in sadness, a situation (very like Lavretsky's) seems 'bleak' and thereby 'requires nothing more from me';[26] in joy the world seems easier to succeed in than usually. We can say, in a word, that the qualities discerned reflect the *salience* of the world to my dealings with it. But two thoughts may then strike one: first, that the world does not appear as salient only when one is emotionally affected; second, that its salience cannot be divorced from the desires one displays in one's dealings. And these thoughts may tempt one back to the picture of emotions as merely derivative from desire. But, before taking up this point, it is worth noting that if the particular kind of salience that emotions disclose is, as Sartre believes, *difficulty*, and if our dealings in the world are, except when utterly smooth or unimportant, replete with difficulty then they will be shot through with emotion as what discloses it. In that case the sharp contrast, assumed by Sartre, between our ordinary commerce with the world and our aberrant emotions will not exist. There will, perhaps, be extreme cases, but our ordinary lives will be lived between them, more or less emotionally.

We turn then to the idea that it is the salience of the world in general that emotions reflect, an idea we have already employed in discussing the affective constitution of our imaginary worlds, whose shape changes with our moods. It is a further idea that emotions mirror the salience the world has for us, not in virtue of our already having desires, but as revealing a world that evokes desire in us precisely because the way the world is shows itself as mattering to us. It is Heidegger, rather than Sartre, who develops these ideas most fruitfully. And it is through analysing the notion of *mood*, rather than of emotion, as Sartre views it, as an agitation, that Heidegger aims to bring out that the way the world matters to us is largely independent of how we would wish it to matter, as measured by our antecedent desires, but, instead, matters to us in a way that makes those desires intelligible. Moods differ from what we can, by contrast, call passions in lacking any determinate object.[27] If my mood is one of depression, for example, I am depressed about things in general, by contrast with being depressed about something in particular – the prevalence of wars, say – while my overall mood may, perhaps, even be buoyant. What Heidegger claims is that it is the possibility of the world as a whole presenting such different faces to us as it does in our different moods that underpins the possibility of our reacting to particular situations as we do.

Here it is worth noticing that passions, as directed to particular objects, are linked to physical reactions in respect of them. I sigh at hearing about yet another war, say, and my reaction is seen by an observer as expressive of my feelings. For me myself, however, I experience the news of war as dolorous, and my involuntary sigh is determinative of how I hear it: I would not have heard it as quite so dolorous without that sigh. Moods, by contrast, are objectless and lack the reactions to specific situations that identify the object of passionate emotions. Our behaviour in them is not, in this sense, reactive. The repeated sighing of this man in a depressed mood, for example, need relate to no specific situations. Yet the depth of his depression, the total cheerlessness of the world as he experiences it, is measured by those sighs.

For Heidegger, moods are absolutely pervasive: we are always in some mood or other.[28] This, he claims, is true of even the apparently most unemotional activity which is the paradigm of purely rational engagement with the world – the theoretical contemplation of nature. For what is necessary to this is a certain kind of *tranquillity*, in which one's investigations are precisely not skewed by irrelevant emotional factors. Yet this tranquillity is one mood among others, others which are often incompatible with this activity. Theoretical activity is, of course, one kind of concern with the world, one way in which it matters to one. But what of complete indifference? Insofar as we have in mind what Heidegger calls 'the pallid lack of mood – indifference which is inclined to do nothing and has no urge for anything', well, this is 'far from nothing at all',[29] it is a mood too, just as numbness in one's fingers – an absence of feeling – is itself a feeling. For an inclination to do nothing is itself a way of dealing with the world which reflects the way it matters to one. In dealing with other people, for example, it manifests itself in perfunctoriness, or even inconsiderateness,[30] because they do not matter as they should.

This gives us a clue as to how Heidegger regards the phenomenon of mood. It is not primarily psychical, in the sense of an inner sense of which we are conscious. We may be quite unconscious of the mood we are in, as in bad moods, Heidegger observes, we are 'blind' to ourselves, even though our mood is very evident to others.[31] Moods are, then, unless deliberately concealed, public, a point Heidegger brings out by observing how the manipulation of shared moods is the province of the orator.[32] Moods are public, and a matter of public interest, because they are primarily states in which we are set to find things in the world mattering to us in one way or another. And it is because, and only because, we find things mattering to us as we do that we are inclined to act in one way or another. People's moods are judged – and, indeed, criticised – on the basis of what they take notice of and respond to, and what they do not. The boss in a bad mood is constantly exasperated by his subordinates' mistakes, of which, in a good mood, he takes no cognisance. It is not that the information, in some supposedly neutral sense, accessed by the one is different from that accessed by the other. 'The world of the happy man is', to borrow Wittgenstein's dictum again, 'a different world from that of the unhappy man', because although there is no neutral sense in which the facts known to them are different, the ways those facts impinge on them and matter are quite at odds. This comes out, in the first instance, in the different ways in which the two men relate to their worlds, and only secondarily in the ways they feel.

The next point to note about moods, on Heidegger's account, is that, as he puts it, we just *find* ourselves in them:[33] they come upon us uninvited, relating us to the world in a way that affects us involuntarily whether with depression, elation or whatever. This is true even when 'through knowledge and will' we become 'master of [our] moods'. For this capacity, by no means always present, can be exercised only 'by way of a counter mood ... we are never free of moods'. Heidegger's point is that to escape from depression, say, is itself something we can attempt only from within a mood that involves non-depressive elements and that it is by exploiting these elements that we may manage to escape into another mood, which itself 'assails' us, if it comes at all.[34] But again this should not be misinterpreted in terms of the essential involuntariness of certain psychical states. What is involuntary is the way we are facing the world and the way things in the world matter to us. The involuntariness of feeling is a consequence of this.

We can, I think, bring out the structure of moods, on Heidegger's conception, without undue dependence on his own particular account of our relation to the world, to which, however, that conception makes an essential contribution. We can do so by developing a little his pronouncement that 'a state of mind always has its understanding ... Understanding always has its mood.'[35] Understanding is, for Heidegger, our fundamental relation to the world and constitutes our capacity to deal with it in any way whatever. As such it has two interdependent aspects. First, to understand the world I am in in any way I need to grasp the opportunities for engagement with it, which it affords. I would completely fail to understand cars, for example, unless I grasped what I might do with one. I need to grasp what possibilities of action are open to me. Second, I need to grasp how the world is relevant to me, how it engages my concerns. I would again fail to understand cars unless I grasped how one driving right towards me might incline me to act.

Both of these aspects of understanding are present in, and require, moods. In depression, for example, my opportunities seem very limited, and limited in particular to producing outcomes in which things get worse rather than better. What is more, the world seems to impinge upon me only as further reducing my prospects or as worsening them. It is in such ways that it affects my understanding of the world. But, conversely, what it is for me to perceive the opportunities I do and what it is for the world to be relevant for me as it is imply that I am in some particular mood. I could not have the kind of understanding of the world implied by the sort of limitation of perceived opportunity or the contraction of appreciation of the world indicated above and fail to be depressed. What it is for the world to matter to us, as any understanding of it requires that it does, *is* for us to be affected by it in the kind of way that moods exemplify, as do those emotions with more determinate objects which we alluded to earlier as passions. Heidegger discerns a relation between moods and such emotions in which moods are, in a way, more basic. What is this relation?

Heidegger's illustration of this relationship is that between anxiety and fear.[36] In the mood of anxiety what I am anxious about is not any definite course of action I do or might engage upon, not, as we expressed it earlier, about some particular opportunities and their outcomes. Rather I am anxious just because I am faced with any opportunities at all, and with the fact that they have outcomes which affect me. Similarly that which occasions anxiety, that in the face of which we are anxious, as Heidegger puts it, is no definite way in which the world is relevant to me: it is the mere fact that it is relevant at all that troubles me. But this, Heidegger observes, is one and the same thing as what I am anxious about;[37] that the world matters and that I must act within it from among the opportunities it offers are two sides of the same coin. To be anxious on account of the latter and about the fact of the former are one and the same. The *analytic* distinction which we have already observed for moods in general makes possible, however, two ways in which the relation to the world manifest in anxiety can become more specific in fear. For fear, Heidegger maintains, is made possible by anxiety and is, indeed, in a sense a species of it.[38]

In the first place, then, what I am fearful about is my *own* predicament (and Heidegger thinks that this referral to oneself is involved even when I am explicitly fearful for others).[39] But what makes me apprehensive is, as he puts it, the prospect of 'the lost present'[40] – not the mere fact that the world confronts me with possibilities, which lies at the root of anxiety, but that in a particular situation it confronts me with the possibility of losing what I have already got, through my own actions or otherwise. It is some feature of this situation that occasions my fear, that in the face of which I am fearful; and it is fearsome because it is, in the way just described, a threat to me. Again it is not the mere fact that the world is relevant which troubles me, as in anxiety, but that it is relevant in just this way, as threatening my situation. So an emotion, like fear, comes about when a mood is, so to speak, made more specific through particular features of the world which furnish it with a determinate object. Yet, Heidegger maintains, such emotions are made possible only because of the existence of indeterminate moods, which pervade one's life even when these emotions are absent. It is only, for example, because of our general fearfulness that fear itself is possible. In both cases the world is presented as mattering to one, and the difference lies only in the specificity – and perhaps urgency or weightiness – of the way it matters.

It is, perhaps, the urgency or weightiness of the demand for action in passionate emotions which explains its further characteristic of involving *feeling*, as general moods may not. Heidegger maintains that, just as moods are not primarily psychical, so emotional experiences which are psychical are possible only in virtue of the sort of understanding of the world which general moods provide. 'Neither of these moods, fear and anxiety', he comments, 'ever "occurs" just isolated in the "Stream of Experiences"; each of them determines an understanding or determines itself in terms of one.'[41] Their possibly experiential character is a derivative feature. Indeed that, in these sorts of cases, the feelings *trouble* me as they do derives from the fact that these states of mind present the world as mattering in a certain way: the feelings trouble me because the world does, and that the world does is, in these cases, manifest in my feelings. It is only because I find myself in such a situation that, as Heidegger puts it, I 'come across "Experiences" at all'.[42] The world can demand action from me urgently or as a matter of great moment only because it can matter to me in certain ways, ways which are manifest in my emotions.

Not only is it emotional experience to which moods are prior, on Heidegger's account: they are also '*prior to* all cognition and volition, and *beyond* their range of disclosure'.[43] This is an ambitious claim, but it follows from Heidegger's account of moods and, if credible, provides a striking answer to some of the questions with which we started this chapter, for it sees emotions, to which moods are fundamental, not as derivative from desires which are frustrated or satisfied, nor yet as a species of cognition in which the significance of happenings in the world is grasped, as well as their supposedly neutral occurrence. Rather the possibility of wanting and willing as well as that of perception are held to depend upon the prevalence of moods. We may consider these two points in order, for they depend upon the two aspects of understanding with which moods provide us, and which we have revisited in the preceding pages in considering anxiety and fear.

First, then, volition, as Heidegger terms this large class of motivational states in which I show preferences among the possibilities apparently open to me. Heidegger discusses willing, wishing, urges and inclinations,[44] but what he says about the first in relation to moods will apply equally to the others. Again Heidegger takes anxiety as a mood which is fundamental in revealing our relation to the world, but, since he draws only upon the general structure of anxiety, it is, rather, the phenomenon of being in some mood or other which he holds to be prior to willing. For, to paraphrase Heidegger, for willing to be possible I must first see myself as confronted with various opportunities and, as an aspect of what he terms 'care', opportunities whose different outcomes matter.[45] There could be no willing of one course of action rather than another except for a creature that viewed itself in this way. But to so view itself it must relate to the world in the way that moods relate us, that is, to have moods itself, like anxiety in the face of the fact that its actions matter. And if one is in such a state of mind, one 'has already got [oneself] into definite possibilities',[46] as Heidegger observes, and that is a pre-condition of choice. Similarly, to will some action in the world, the world must show itself as a place where what happens, including the results of my action, matters (another aspect of care). Again this requires, as we have already seen, the existence of a mood which relates us to the world as mattering in this way, so that things in it, in respect of which we act, are useful, harmful and so on, as our mood reveals.

Heidegger mounts a precisely analogous defence of the claim that moods are prior to cognition – again a broad category, including sensory perception and thinking generally as well as knowledge proper.[47] We noticed near the beginning of this section that Heidegger believes that even the most theoretical contemplation of the world involves a mood. What he now seeks to show is that our thought and perception of the world is partly determined by our mood, so that mood does not merely colour what is already given but is what makes it possible for it to be discovered by us at all. Thus 'in fearing ... we do not first ascertain a future evil ... and then fear it ... fearing ... discovers it beforehand in its fearsomeness'.[48] A ferocious beast before us, for example, is not first perceived as such, and thus judged dangerous. Those cognitions are secondary to our reacting fearfully to it, and that we perceive it sensorily at all, Heidegger claims, depends upon such emotional reactions and, therefore, on the moods in which they can occur:

> Only because the 'senses' belong ontologically to an entity whose kind of Being is Being-in-the-world with a state-of-mind, can they be 'touched' by anything or 'have a sense for' something in such a way that what touches them shows itself as an affect.[49]

Heidegger goes on to argue that 'all sight' – in which he includes all sensory perception – 'is grounded primarily in understanding', which, we may recall, itself 'always has its mood'. This, as he puts it, deprives 'pure intuition of its priority'.[50] Rather, because we are concerned with what is possible for us and with how the world is relevant to that, we see things, and think of them, in the light of those concerns, which, because mood is prior to volition, are basically concerns we find ourselves with, rather than ones we shape for ourselves. I see the thing speeding towards me on the road as a car, for example, and avoid it, without any intervening process of seeing an object of a certain shape, size and motion or of inferring what it is and what to do. But, as we have noted, I can do this just because I can be in the appropriate mood – one of caution, say – a mood that alerts me to the possibility of various things appearing, which, were I not cautious, I would not be heedful of as these things, with the potential to affect me that they do. Except in the most extreme cases of recklessness or indifference I cannot but be concerned about them, and such concerns are evident, too, in my planning and even in apparently disinterested thinking about my world. Emotions, and moods more particularly, play, then, for Heidegger, an absolutely fundamental role in what it is to be a subject of thought and experience about the world. It is the salience of the world to all my thought and action that emotions reflect, and they do so by evoking desires, not as a result of pre-existing ones.

Feeling and the Body

Heidegger's account of emotions is a very attractive one. But readers will have noticed one aspect of emotions with which Sartre is crucially concerned that is apparently completely absent from it, namely, the way in which bodily reactions are involved in emotions, providing us with a view of the world, and how those reactions are necessary for the feelings through which this view can strike us. Indeed, Heidegger's emphasis on moods, rather than passions, and his denial that moods are primarily psychical, may seem to suggest that there can be no essential role for bodily reactions and their concomitant feelings within his framework. This would, we think, be a mistaken conclusion to draw. In fact Heidegger does touch upon bodily reactions. In fear, he says, 'one shrinks back in the face of something',[51] and he has a bodily reaction in mind even if he intends this partly as a metaphor. But not only in fear, in anxiety too one shrinks back, though this time the whole set of the body towards one's situation in the world is connoted. Indeed, it would be curious if Heidegger did not have bodily reactions in mind when writing of moods, partly since he totally rejects the Cartesian picture of human beings as mere compounds of mind and body, and seeks to show how this rests on a misunderstanding of both,[52] partly because his stress on the involuntariness of moods is connected with our bodily existence: 'anxiety', he notes, 'is often conditioned by 'physiological factors',[53] but this is possible, he goes on, only because of the sort of creatures we are, with our capacity for being ill at ease in the world.

This last point directs us towards a better understanding of Heidegger's apparent, but only apparent, downgrading of *feelings* in his discussion of mood. In fact it is not feeling as such that Heidegger is rejecting as essential to moods, but rather a false picture of feeling *as* purely psychical, so that again a relationship to bodily reaction is suggested rather than excluded. What Heidegger rejects is the Cartesian idea of feelings as events accessible to reflection even without reference to the subject's environment. So, for example, Heidegger denies that the different ways in which fear may be felt are 'degrees of "feeling tones"'.[54] Instead, they constitute alarm if one is suddenly threatened, dread if what threatens is unfamiliar, and terror if both. The difference in feeling is, then, a difference in how the world presents itself, not something intrinsic to mental events. Nonetheless, even when this defence of Heidegger has been mounted the fact remains that he does little to illuminate the way that the body is involved in a world being presented to the subject.

For that we can turn, perhaps, to the work of the French psychoanalyst and philosopher Julia Kristeva. Kristeva throughout her work characterises a variety of moods and more specific emotions in terms of the bodily reactions they involve and the way these connect with our feelings towards things. A key example occurs in her seminal work *Powers of Horror*:

> Loathing an item of food, a piece of filth, waste, or dung. The spasms and vomitings that protect me. The repugnance, the retching that thrusts me to the side ... The fascinated start that leads me toward and separates me from them.[55]

The mixed emotion of repulsion and fascination evinced in these reactions is, Kristeva maintains, characteristic of what she describes as *abjection*, an attitude in which things are simultaneously repudiated and yet held on to. Kristeva traces this attitude back pyschoanalytically to a primal repression in which the child breaks out of its original experience of unity with the mother and begins to establish an independent identity. Abjection is the throwing out of an original part of one whose physical manifestation is the spitting out of the mother's milk, so that 'food loathing is perhaps the most elementary and most archaic form of abjection'.[56] It is this act of abjection, constantly repeated in other forms, which Kriesteva sees as necessary to maintain the boundaries of the self and to prevent it being swamped by what is beyond it.

The notion of abjection provides Kristeva with a tool for diagnosing a number of puzzling emotional responses, but she does so through appealing to their physical manifestations as much as to their phenomenological character. This is not only because, like Freud, she sees them as expressions of drives that are opaque to their subjects, but also because she exploits a feature of Heidegger's account which we have not so far mentioned – the propensity of those afflicted by moods like anxiety to turn away from what it unsettlingly reveals about one's place in the world and seek refuge in the familiar.[57] For Kristeva the analyst, then, the task is to diagnose, on the basis of physical symptoms, feelings unacknowledged by their subjects, and to expose the relation to the world that they manifest. What makes this a phenomenological task, rather than a purely Freudian one involving an appeal to occult mechanisms, is that the subject can be brought to see what that relation is by reflecting upon her feelings, and for that the story of a primal repression is, in fact, otiose.

Kristeva brings to this task an account, albeit sketchy, of how our bodily reactions relate us to a world revealed to feeling. The account starts with moods, which lack determinate objects and thus relate us to an undifferentiated world, or rather we are 'deprived of world',[58] in the sense of an area for meaningful activity, so that in depression, say, we find it hard to act, and in euphoria we act just for the sake of acting. But what characterises moods is their involuntary physical manifestations, which can often be experienced as bodily sensations and which always mediate the way things seem to one. In depression, for example, I am gripped by lethargy, 'my rhythm slowed down', as is as apparent to others as to myself; but it is through this lethargy that it appears that 'my existence is on the verge of collapsing, its lack of meaning ... obvious to me, glaring, inescapable'.[59] Such moods are expressed in the way that, as Kristeva puts it, 'discrete quantities of energy move through the body of the subject',[60] that is to say, by semiotic rather than symbolic features of behaviour. Thus 'literary creation ... transposes affect into rhythms, signs, forms'[61] and it is the non-symbolic aspects of language that constitute the semiotic and which are the primary vehicles for expressing mood. In, for example, the lines,

> Break, break, break,
> On thy cold gray stones, O Sea[62]

it is the sluggishness of the rhythm that conveys the poet's despondency. 'On the frontier between animality and symbol formation', Kristeva suggests, 'moods – and particularly sadness – are the ultimate reactions to our traumas, they are our basic homeostatic recourses'. But she goes on, no doubt with literature and art in mind, 'a diversification of moods, variety in sadness, refinement in sorrow or mourning are the imprint of a humankind that is ... subtle, ready to fight, and creative'.[63]

Although Kristeva does not explicitly raise the question of how emotions with determinate objects, passions, differ from moods, one can see how she might, perhaps, begin to answer it. Is it that in such emotions we have crossed the border into the symbolic? That is to say, that the patterns of behaviour exhibited in a specific situation serve to relate their agent to determinate features of it, and to a range of determinate outcomes, in a way that can only be mapped by symbolic processes? But if we adopt such an approach have we not reverted to the sort of cognitivism whose deficiences we noted earlier, in particular its incapacity to account for the way our bodily reactions, and the feelings to which they commonly give rise, are not just an adjunct to the actions explained by the way we see the world in an emotion but a necessary feature of this way of seeing it?

Kristeva's response would seem to be that we would only grasp the point of emotional behaviour – to escape in fear, hit back in anger, revel in joy and so on – if it was genuinely reactive.[64] But that is to say that in it the body must be afflicted, with all its concomitant sensations. Yet these must be experienced not just as bodily sensations which affect one, as in physical illness, but as sensory states through which I discern features of the world that matter to me. If these different aspects of emotion come apart then we are left with a variety of pathological conditions that it is, Kristeva would maintain, the business of the psychoanalyst to treat. How they are to be treated is, however, irrelevant to the argument here. For the purpose of treatment is to reconnect the different aspects – to render feeling meaningfully expressible in the case of autism, say, or to bring feeling back to 'discourse [that] was numbed' in some cases of depression.[65] And, unless these aspects of emotion are brought together, their associated behaviour and symptoms are likely to be unintelligible, not only to others but to their subjects.

This picture allows us to see, like Sartre, the desires that arise from an emotion as distinctive of it and not otherwise intelligible. But, unlike Sartre, it does not view them as thereby contrasting with the supposedly ordinary desires that explain rational action. No doubt many cerebral desires, far removed, as it were, from the well springs of action in our immediate reactions to the world, are unemotional enough. Yet, Kristeva argues, the desires that shape our responses to that world, and thus reveal our sense of what it is like and how we would have it be, need to be charged with affect to be intelligible. The traditional distinction, reproduced by Sartre, between emotional and rational action therefore breaks down. Insofar as it exists, it does so at the level of mood versus emotion directed at determinate objects. For, while the behaviour manifest in moods does exhibit its agent's view of the world, it does not do so by demonstrating what could be a reasoned response to it. It is, however, as Heidegger shows, precisely the sort of capacities to be affected by the world revealed in moods that make possible responses that are both rational and emotional.

Summary

The principal problem in understanding emotions is to see how their affective aspect – the way they make us feel and react physically – fits together with their cognitive aspect – the way they present us with a particular view of the world. On the one hand, physical reactions and sensations may seem to have nothing to do with representing the world in a certain way; on the other, no way of representing the world may seem essentially to require such reactions and sensations. Yet, somehow, in emotion both are inextricably involved.

Sartre makes the connection by regarding emotional reactions as a substitute for purposive behaviour when the world is too 'difficult' for that to be effective. But these 'difficulties' are not grasped unemotionally and, as a consequence of this, reacted to non-rationally. Rather the difficulties in question are the emotive features of the world, not accessible otherwise than through reactions of the body whose capacities they challenge. While this last point is persuasive, however, Sartre's sharp distinction between rational purposive activity and emotional behaviour needs to be questioned.

Heidegger, who influenced Sartre in many other respects, does not draw this sharp distinction. Rather, Heidegger takes the view that purposive activity, as well as passionately emotional behaviour, is made possible only because our engagement with the world is pervaded by *moods* which come over us involuntarily. Moods reveal the features of the world in virtue of which what we do matters to us in the way it does. That the world is a fearful place, for example, is what makes me cautious, and it is what makes it possible for me to be frightened by some specific thing in the world. None of this requires, and Sartre would concur in this, any prior desires, for safety say. For such desires are intelligible only given the way our moods reveal the world as mattering to us.

The lacuna in Heidegger's account is the role of bodily reactions and sensations in emotions. Arguably this gap can be filled by reference to considerations adduced by Julia Kristeva. Kristeva sees moods as bodily affects, operating in the realm of the 'semiotic' – the pre-symbolic – since they lack determinate objects. But emotions directed at such objects, and hence affording cognition through symbols, must also involve similar physical reactions and sensations or else it would be unintelligible why the specific features in the world that they discern should matter to us in the way they do. For it is our bodies that register, normally or pathologically, the way the world matters to us, prior to any deliberation on our part as to how it should.

Notes

1. See Donald Davidson, *Essays on Actions and Events* (Oxford: Clarendon Press, 1980), pp. 3–19. This is not, however, the picture of explanation which we adopt here: see Chapter 6.
2. Ivan S. Turgenev, *Liza* (London: Dent, 1914), pp. 75–6.
3. See David Hume, *A Treatise of Human Nature* (1739–40, many editions), Book III.
4. Jean-Paul Sartre, *Sketch for a Theory of the Emotions* (London: Methuen, 1971), p. 66.
5. Ibid., p. 78.
6. Ibid., p. 67.
7. Ibid., p. 88.
8. Ibid., p. 90.
9. Richard Wollheim, *On the Emotions* (New Haven: Yale University Press, 1999), p. 83.
10. Ibid., p. 87.
11. Ibid., pp. 89–90.
12. Sartre, *Sketch*, p. 65.
13. Ibid., p. 63.
14. Ibid., p. 82.
15. Ibid., p. 63 (our italics).
16. Wollheim, *On the Emotions*, p. 86.
17. Sartre, *Sketch*, p. 71.
18. L. Wittgenstein, *Tractatus Logico-Philosophicus* (London: Routledge, 1961), 6.43.
19. Sartre, *Sketch*, pp. 56–8.
20. See Wollheim, *On the Emotions*, pp. 17, 28, 61. There are emotions which do depend upon pre-existing desires, e.g. disappointment, but others, e.g. love, do not.
21. Sartre, *Sketch*, p. 67.
22. Ibid., p. 72.
23. Ibid., pp. 76–7.
24. Ibid., pp. 84–5.
25. By Paul E. Griffiths, in 'Basic Emotions, Complete Emotions, Machiavellian Emotions', in A. Hatzimoysis (ed.), *Philosophy and the Emotions* (Cambridge: Cambridge University Press, 2003), pp. 59–60.
26. Sartre, *Sketch*, p. 69.
27. Heidegger uses the notion of mood rather more widely, applying it to emotions with determinate objects like fear, but he generally distinguishes these from moods proper as 'affects'.
28. Martin Heidegger, *Being and Time* (Oxford: Blackwell, 1967), H 134.
29. Ibid., H 345, 134.
30. Cp. ibid., H 123.
31. Ibid., H 136.
32. Ibid., H 138–9.

33. Ibid., H 135.
34. Ibid., H 136.
35. Ibid., H 142-3.
36. In fact anxiety plays a crucial role in *Being and Time* as the fundamental mood, reflecting our basic relation to the world, but in later works this claim is dropped and anxiety may be viewed as just one mood among others in which our relation to the world is exemplified.
37. Ibid., H 140, 186, 188.
38. Ibid., H 186, 189.
39. Ibid., H 141-2.
40. Ibid., H 344-5.
41. Ibid., H 344.
42. Ibid., H 136.
43. Ibid., H 136.
44. Ibid., H 182, 194.
45. Heidegger views 'care' as constituting human existence. See ibid., H 57, 121-2. Mood and understanding are interdependent aspects of what it is to exist in the world, and care may be viewed as bringing these together into a single relationship to it. For further development, see Chapter 6.
46. Ibid., H 144.
47. Ibid., H 147.
48. Ibid., H 141.
49. Ibid., H 137.
50. Ibid., H 147. This point has been discussed above in Chapter 1.
51. Ibid., H 185.
52. E.g. ibid., H 48, 56, 368.
53. Ibid., H 190.
54. Ibid., H 142.
55. Kelly Oliver (ed.), *The Portable Kristeva* (New York: Columbia University Press, 1997), p. 230.
56. Ibid., p. 230.
57. See Heidegger, *Being and Time*, H 186-9. Note the resemblance to Sartre's account here.
58. Oliver, *Kristeva*, p. 231.
59. Ibid., pp. 180-1.
60. Ibid., p. 201 n. 24.
61. Ibid., p. 193.
62. Alfred Lord Tennyson, *Poetical Works* (London: Oxford University Press, 1953), p. 116.
63. Oliver, *Kristeva*, p. 193. Note that Kristeva does not hold that semiotic effects are achieved only through natural rather than cultural processes, which utilise conventions to determine what is to count as such effects.
64. We extrapolate from Kristeva's general claim that the symbolic aspect of language needs to be linked to its semiotic or affective ones if it is to have a point in expressing the communicative intentions of a speaker.
65. Ibid., pp. 123, 218.

6

Reason, Agency and Understanding

Reason and Culture

In the previous chapter our discussion of emotion drew attention to an often made contrast between intentional engagements with the world, explicable in terms of reason, and emotional responses, themselves bodily, which apparently fall outside the sphere of purposive, intentional engagement. This contrast worked on a picture of intentional action which involved mental deliberation and the operation of impersonal standards of reasoning, and a picture of emotion as disruptive bodily eruptions of a personal kind which assail otherwise rational subjects. By the end of the chapter, however, this contrast had been undermined, by an account of our bodily emotional responses as revealing the shape our world has for us. Emotions disclose our imaginary world. Consequently Sartre's sharp distinction between rational purposive activity and emotional behaviour is questioned. Both intentional engagement and emotional responses require an imaginary shape to our world, a shape constituted, for Heidegger, by the mood which frames it.

In this chapter we will be looking at the model of reason and agency which has informed that sharp distinction. This chapter traces the move from an intellectualist model of agency, informed by deliberation employing impersonal and universal methods of reasoning, to a conception of engaged agency, whose rationality is immanent within the experiences of embodied agents within the world. Such rationality is not, however, simply personal.

It does not derive from the characteristics of individual subjects. As Heidegger emphasises, we find ourselves in a world of significance, which is 'always already' there. Such 'thrown-ness' is the condition of being a subject at all. There is no prior subject who then projects significance on to the world. We are subjects only in virtue of experiencing a world which matters to us.

The imaginary shape of our world, which makes possible projective projects within it, is one into which we are initiated by culture, (*Bildung*).[1] This process is discussed here in an attempt to resolve three problems which it appears to face. One is the problem of conservatism. How do changes come in our ways of understanding our worlds? The second is the question of reflective and critical thinking. If we are initiated into ways of experiencing, which become *second nature*[2] to us, what space is there for critical reflection? The third issue confronts difference. Given differences within and across cultures, as well as within different aspects of ourselves, how can we understand different ways of experiencing and rationally evaluate them? These are the questions which this chapter will be addressing.

Reason and Action: the Classical Picture

There is a widespread consensus within contemporary analytic philosophy circles regarding the distinction between bodily movement and action. What marks our intentional engagement with the world is the susceptibility of such acts to explanation in terms of reasons. There is also a wide consensus on what counts as a reason for acting. Classically an agent has a reason to perform a certain kind of action when she has (1) a pro attitude towards some end or objective, and (2) a belief that an action of that kind will promote that end. In contemporary literature the term 'pro attitude' derives from the work of Donald Davidson. It includes 'desires, wantings, urges, promptings, and a great variety of moral views and aesthetic principles',[3] states, that is, which provide us with goals or objectives towards which our actions are directed. It is common to use the term desire as a generic term for such pro attitudes.

The reason giving relation between an agent's intentional states and her actions is usually spelt out by the construction of sequences of practical reasoning. Reasons for actions and reasons for beliefs are thereby seen as analogous. Both are viewed as essentially calculations, or arguments, in support of a conclusion. The construction of theoretical reasoning, where an agent has reasons for belief, is done by making evident inductive or deductive relations between contents of beliefs already held and the new belief. In the case of reasons for actions, where one of the reason providing states is a desire, the construction of the reasoning is less straightforward and the subject of much debate. However something like the following schema is usually suggested whenever an agent has a reason for acting.

P1: G is desirable
P2: Xing is a way to G
Conclusion: Xing is a good idea.
(I would like the doctor to come. Ringing the bell will bring him. Ringing the bell would be a good idea.)

Presenting this in a formal way makes clear that specification of the goal must appear in P1 and P2 and of the behaviour in P2 and the Conclusion. Reason is then instrumental reason, calculating means to achieve pre-given ends.

In both the theoretical and the practical case, therefore, the construction of reasons requires representations. The states of affairs desired or believed are represented to the agent and captured propositionally in the construction of reasoning. The reason giving relation is then primarily a relation between representations. The presence of a reason for acting or believing does not necessarily make it rational for an agent to believe or act in that way. She may have other beliefs that provide conflicting evidence or have conflicting desires. To establish what it is rational overall to believe or do we would need to establish principles for assessing competing probabilities and weighting competing goals. These are formalised in probability calculus and decision theory. Such accounts require initial beliefs and desires, which can form the content of such reasoning and from which, in a rational way, further beliefs and desires can be derived. The beliefs are thought of as deriving from perceptual experiences or in some cases given a priori. The initial desires are similarly thought of as causally, but not rationally, given.

On this account to have a reason for believing or acting is to be attributable sequences of explicit or implicit reasoning, which employ valid methods to reach conclusions about what is most likely to be true or what it is best to do. To be irrational is to make mistakes in this sequence of reasoning or, without good enough reason, to act or to believe contrary to its conclusions. What sequences of argument count as valid or rational is determined in terms of universal principles, which, it is normally assumed, are susceptible to formal articulation, principles of inductive and deductive reasoning, in the case of belief, and (more problematically) principles governing rational decision-making, in the case of intention and action. To be rational is to hold your beliefs for good reasons and act in a way that will maximise the chances of achieving your goals. These principles of good reasoning are taken to govern the workings of the mind. Human beings are to greater or lesser extent rational. They are capable of lapses, of believing something when they have evidence against it, or acting in ways they know will not best promote their goals. There is, however, a limit on how severe these lapses can be if a creature is to be attributed beliefs, desires and other intentional states at all. On this picture to explain someone's belief or action by providing a reason for it is, at least in part (see below), to *justify* it. It is to show that it was an appropriate thing to do or to believe in those circumstances. The normativity here is directly related to the satisfaction of norms. It is to show that the beliefs or actions were in line with universal norms of rationality.

This classical conception of reason and its accompanying account of intentional action is shared by writers with very different accounts of the relation between mind and body. For Descartes, reasoning was an activity of a subject directing an essentially mechanical body by means of an act of will. Where such direction seems absent, for example, when an action has become habitual, as in walking, it ceased to count as an action and fell into the realm of a bodily movement explained exclusively in terms of mechanical causation. Within contemporary materialism the body is playing quite a different role. The structures of reason giving explanation, which mark us as intentional agents, are to be reduced themselves to the operations of mechanical causation. In the most developed version of such a reduction, the language of thought theory, desires and beliefs are inner physical states of a system whose reason-giving relations are reduced to patterns of causal relations consequent on syntactic features of their instantiation.[4] Here the need for a directing subject or indeed a subject of any kind has disappeared. A rational system is one that manifests certain kinds of causal patterns. This is the view that then informs computer models of the mind. For, in a move that clearly separates rationality from any considerations of subjectivity, a computer too can be rational, for it can be constructed to operate on rational principles. The conception of rationality as the instantiation of sequences of objectively specifiable patterns is also found in contemporary accounts which reject the intentional realism of language of thought models. For interpretationalists, such as Dennett and Davidson, to be a rational system is to be interpretable by a third party as a rational system,[5] that is, for objective patterns to be detectable in your behavioural response to your environment. These patterns are not causal ones, but aid interaction and prediction. Once again there is no link with subjectivity. The patterns are simply a cloak of interpretation thrown by third persons over the behaviour of an essentially mechanistic body. In all of these accounts reason itself remains specifiable in a universal way. Rational agents are those who conform to its non-perspectival tenets.

Problems with the Classical Account

Despite the ubiquitous nature of the account of reason and agency offered above, it has been subject to a number of criticisms. One of these criticisms concerns the difficulties of specifying in a formal and general way what constitutes a good practical or theoretical argument. John McDowell has made the claim that there is 'no mechanical test for logical validity in general'.[6] The rationality of a belief rests on its relation to a network, without rigid boundaries, of other beliefs. Furthermore John Searle, in an argument which will prove central to the rest of this chapter, points out that the rationality of the relations between our intentional states rests not only on other intentional states but also on sets of background capacities, practices and know-how which inform our responses on a particular occasion. Such background practices cannot be made explicit.[7]

Searle's problems here are connected to issues which arise when we consider Wittgenstein's discussion of rule following. However a rule is expressed, according to Wittgenstein, it leaves open a number of ways in which it could be applied.[8] These different interpretations cannot be reduced by the adding of further caveats to the rules, which themselves would be open to multiple interpretations. The only way in which ambiguity can be eliminated is by agreement in practices. We each apply the rules in ways in which our communities can recognise and agree is appropriate. There are different ways in which such a resolution can be interpreted. One is to see such agreement as a result of causal conditioning by society or the hard wiring of our brain.[9] Here the question of whether one way of applying the rule is more rational than another simply does not arise. Another interpretation is that, in a given context, agreement in practices reflects a shared 'grasp on things'[10] which, although it may not be articulable, makes the application an intelligible and rational one. 'Following arrows towards the point is not just an arbitrarily imposed connection: it makes sense, granted the way arrows move.'[11] But such agreement is an agreement in practice, anchored in specific contexts of application.

A different problem has been highlighted by John McDowell. It concerns the *givenness* of the beliefs and desires which form the premises of such reasoning. For McDowell such desires and beliefs cannot themselves be justified, if they are simply caused by outer stimulus or inner turmoil. We take our beliefs to be rationally answerable to a world by adjusting themselves to our experiences of it. But such experiences cannot provide reasons for beliefs and desires unless they themselves already have a content which yields justificatory relations to other beliefs and to appropriate forms of behaviour. McDowell points out that our experiences of our world do have just such a content, one which constitutively links them to appropriate responses and further beliefs. Their justificatory relations are therefore immanent to the content of the experiences.[12] (For McDowell such content must be conceptual, a demand he interprets as implying linguistic articulation, but such a move will not be assumed here.)

McDowell's position links to a further problem with the account of rationality offered above, for such an impersonal account fails to capture the experience of rationality from the point of view of the subject. It provides us with the observer's relation to an act rather than the agent's relation. This point is somewhat difficult to tease out. On the account of rationality explored it was recognised that pointing to the rationality of an action or belief was a distinctive way of making the outcome intelligible. It was made intelligible by showing that it was the correct, or a correct, response. The notion of correctness, however, was spelt out here in terms of conformity to objectively characterisable norms. That the behaviour of the agent conforms, to the extent that it does, to such norms is then further explained by the fact that it is a constitutive feature of rational subjects to act or believe on rational considerations, or, by the apparently contingent causal or interpretive fact, that we are the kind of creatures that rationality moves or whose patterns of behaviour can be interpreted rationally. This fact is then sometimes further explained by a turn to evolutionary considerations. The particularity of the subject is involved only in providing the specific goals and beliefs, which can then be fed into the sequences of reasoning. On this picture there is no difference between explaining the behaviour of a person and the behaviour of a rationally programmed computer. This kind of story, however, fails to accommodate the point of view of the agent. It fails to incorporate how, for the agent, an action strikes them as the thing or a thing to do. Yet it is grasp of the situation from the agent's point of view that we need to have if we are to understand the action, and not simply see it as an instance of a regularity, causal or otherwise. To gain such understanding requires what McDowell calls 'a sensitivity to the specific detail of the subjective stance of another'.[13] We need to know how the world appears from their point of view. When we grasp their experience of the world, certain actions show up as appropriate or inappropriate within it. If from your point of view someone looks to have been hurt, then it thereby appears appropriate to help them. When the garden looks sunny and inviting, it thereby looks appropriate to go into it. The perception is *already* motivational and does not need supplementing by some further goal to make it so. We can make the action intelligible by grasping the experiences the agent has of the world.

To summarise: on the account of intentional agency under consideration such agency is seen as marked by the availability of reason-giving explanations. To act for a reason, then, is to act to fulfil previously given goals, via a calculus of means and ends. This account sees the rationality of a system as its conformity to objectively specifiable norms of reasoning. The account runs into problems, however, in trying to specify these norms objectively. Any such specification remains indeterminate until anchored in specific practices, within a context. Moreover any specification implicitly rests on a background of assumptions and know-how which can never be made fully explicit. Rationality, rather than the application of general norms to concrete situations, seems to reside within practices and specific contexts. Furthermore the impersonal account of rationality makes contingent any link between intentional engagement in the world and subjectivity. Subjects who constitutively have a point of view on the world are not required for intentional agency. What gets lost is a mode of recognising engaged agency as a reflection of just such a subjective view. These two groups of problems are interconnected with a view of the body found within the impersonal account. Either the body is a mechanical clock to be set ticking by the input from a rationally structured subject or it becomes the material medium of such rational structuring. In either case the body is simply an object in the world rather than the embodiment of a point of view within it.

Bodily Engagements

McDowell's recognition that the content of our perceptual experiences are constitutively linked to judgements and agency, and, in his terms, already part of the sphere of *spontaneity*, links his views to the phenomenological writers discussed in Chapter 1. We have already discussed how our perceptions of the world are, in Heidegger's terms, perceptions of the world as 'ready to hand'. We perceive hammers and chairs and suitcases, a world as apt for our projects within it.[14]

As we discussed in Chapter 1, within phenomenological writings an intellectualist account of intentional agency is rejected in favour of a picture of a bodily engagement with the world, which is necessary for and more basic than explicit deliberation. Heidegger discusses this form of engagement with the use of the term 'understanding'. For Heidegger understanding is a mode of being in the world in which the world is revealed as a potentiality for engagement. Understanding in this account is not a cognitive activity, but more like a form of 'know-how', a way of conducting ourselves towards the world. 'With the term "understanding" we have in mind a fundamental existentiale, which is neither a definite species of cognition distinguished, let us say, from explaining and conceiving, nor any cognition at all in the sense of grasping something thematically.' For Heidegger, 'all explanation is ... rooted in ... primary understanding'.[15]

This mode of conducting ourselves has the character of 'projection', 'press(ing) forward into possibilities'. These possibilities do not exist as representations in an inner consciousness but are revealed in the way the world is experienced by us and our 'comportment' within it.

> Projection has nothing to do with ... a plan that has been thought out ... the character of understanding as projection is such that the understanding does not grasp thematically that upon which it projects, that is to say possibilities. Grasping it in such a manner would take away from what is projected its very character as a possibility, and would reduce it to the given contents which we have in mind.[16]

What possibilities the world shows to us is consequent on our situation within it. Heidegger is insistent here that the possibilities he is concerned with are neither logical possibilities nor ones which are empirically possible. What show up for us as possibilities for action reflect our situatedness. We have suggested in previous chapters that the world we experience is an imaginary world, structured with affect, in the light of which certain actions show up as desirable and undesirable. This, which Heidegger would term affectedness, is part, but not all, of what show up for us as possible courses of action. Not everything it might be desirable to do is possible to do. Opportunities, for example, might not lie near at hand. What shows up, as a possibility to do, requires both a local and general background which can never be made fully explicit, but which constitutes the context and situation in which we act. The context here includes cultural context (of which more below). Dreyfus gives an example to illustrate Heidegger's point here.

> If Heidegger's carpenter sees that it is lunch time, it is logically possible for him to eat rocks, and physically possible for him to eat acorns. He could also arbitrarily choose not to eat at all and go fishing. However, given his cultural background, his current mood ... and current involvement in his work, only a certain range of possibilities, say knackwurst or bratwurst, are actually available to him.[17]

The background is not something of which I am focally aware when seeing the possibilities of a situation. It is nonetheless what makes certain choices make sense to me.

When we turned our attention to the work of Merleau-Ponty it became clear that the kind of comportment, which Heidegger terms understanding, is a form of *bodily* engagement with the world. Merleau-Ponty argues for a mode of intentional engagement with the world which conforms neither to the intellectualist picture of a body being directed by a rational subject, nor to the mechanistic picture, of behaviour as the outcome of mechanical causation. Instead the body itself is conceived of as that which has know-how of its world, manifest in its successful negotiation of its environment without the necessity for prior deliberation. As we made clear in Chapter 1, for Merleau-Ponty knowledge of our environment is, at its most basic, *practical* knowledge, not knowledge by description. 'Movement is not thought about movement, and bodily space [the space of action] is not space thought of or represented'.[18] The possibility of other kinds of knowledge rests on these practical abilities.

> In order to be able to assert a truth, the actual subject must in the first place have a world or be in the world, that is sustain round about it a system of meanings whose reciprocities, relationships and involvements do not need to be made explicit in order to be exploited. When I move about my house, I know, without thinking about it, that walking towards the bathroom means passing near to the bedroom, that looking at the window means having the fireplace on my left, and in this small world each gesture, each perception, is immediately located in relation to a great number of possible coordinates ... My flat is, for me, not a set of closely associated images. It remains a familiar domain round about me only as long as I still have 'in my hands' and 'in my legs' the main distances and directions involved, and as long as my body's intentional threads run out towards it.[19]

The lack of explicit representation of the world, in this process, in no way reduces the activities involved to that of mechanical causation, as was assumed by Descartes. This practical know-how is not a reflex movement. It requires an awareness of the subject of a unified body and world. We discussed in Chapter 3 the need for a corporeal schema or body image to inform our interaction with our environment. This image does not, however, require explicit conceptualisation or linguistic expression. It is not an inner representation but a mode of awareness of a corporeal entity. This schema is not simply a reflection of present position but is open to future possibilities. Our body image, or corporeal schema, is framed in terms of potentialities for engagement, and thereby is interdependently a mode of awareness of our world. 'Consciousness is being-towards-the-thing through the intermediary of the body.'[20] In this context the habitual actions discussed in Chapter 1 become central. The acquisition of a habit is a problem for both intellectualist and mechanistic accounts. Habitual actions proceed without deliberation and are commonly learnt without explicit instructions, often by copying and mimicking others. They are not, however, mechanistic, for the situations requiring the habit are physically quite diverse and require the recognition by the subject of a common significance to bring the habitual response into play. 'The grasping of a habit is indeed the grasping of a significance, but it is the motor grasping of a motor significance.'[21]

Merleau-Ponty contrasts the habitual body, knowingly finding its way around its environment, with the intellectualist one, by considering pathological cases. He discusses the case of a man called Schneider who has lost such spontaneous engagement with the world. Schneider when asked about the position of his body needs to observe it as an object in space. He does not seek or initiate movement, but when given an order tries until his body fits a form which he recognises. 'The order has an intellectual significance to him and not a motor one.'[22] Although able to make judgements about the world in representational form, Schneider has lost his world in the sense of this term to which both Heidegger and Merleau-Ponty are drawing our attention. No longer is it experienced by him as a field of potentiality. His experiences of it give him no reasons to respond. Our habitual negotiation of our world is not a brute causal response to a material stimulus. It requires modes of awareness, integrated body/world images or schemas. However, these are not necessarily mediated by representations which can be slotted into sequences of reasoning. In response to intellectualisation in the work of Kant, Merleau-Ponty insists that the synthesising of experience, required if there is to be a world for a subject, is essentially a practical, not an intellectual, activity.

The emphasis on the role played by pre-reflective understanding in the work of both Heidegger and Merleau-Ponty does not, however, rule out the importance of language. For these writers language is a primary vehicle by which we are initiated into having a world (of which more below). Language, however, does not have a primarily representative function. It rather serves to extend the possibility of engaged agency. Words are uttered as a part of our activities in dealing with things ready to hand. I may say, 'Hand me the other hammer', when this one is found to be too heavy. It is in such uses, rather than in assertions, that simply describe the world, that Heidegger, like Wittgenstein, finds the primary use of language. The world therefore is not thought of in terms of the subject matter of shared representations, which a set of assertions might express. Rather, it is a place we live in. Linguistic articulation makes visible new possibilities, shapes the world in different ways and consequently suggests new possibilities of response. The language we use in the business of life itself consists of things ready to hand. They are perceived as meaningful on account of the particular context of activity within which they are used. Language then is structured as a consequence of the uses to which it has been put, and this structure allows it to span many different activities.

There are, moreover, cases when the calculative account of rationality finds a place. Our unreflective interactions often meet obstacles, which require us to conceptualise the features of a situation explicitly. Or our projective possibilities are long term and require careful planning. Even in these cases, however, the possibility of such reasoning makes sense only against a context and background of engaged agency of the kind outlined above. Furthermore, the process of planning often proceeds not by sequences of reasoning but by exercises of the imagination. In his discussion of what he terms the 'practical imaginary', Ricoeur argues that 'it is in the realm of the imaginary that I try out my capacity to do something, that I take the measure of "I can"'.[23]

We must be careful, nonetheless, not to draw too firm a boundary between the theoretical (concerned with making judgements) and the practical. This might suggest a realm of practical activity, structured by pre-reflective meanings, encompassed in bodily responses to the world, separated from a realm of theoretical activity, with its explicitly articulated representations, governed by just the kind of norms of rationality which we started out by discussing. The problem with this picture is two way. It is not just, as we have argued above, that the theoretical activity requires and only makes sense in the context of practical know-how, informed by situated experiences and background. It is also important to recognise that the pre-reflective meanings informing our bodily engagements often derive from the more explicit theoretical beliefs of current or past communities. Mohanty, for example, argues

> There is continuing 'communication' between theoretical and practical meaning systems ... there is pre-reflective but theoretical meaning just as there is reflective practice ... one tends to posit a phase of mankind's (or society's) life which is purely practical, uncontaminated by any theoretical thinking, where there is only knowing-how, but no knowing-that, so that the emergence of theoretical thinking is seen as a threat to the integrity of that seamless practical life. This is, I think, a mistake ... a romantic positing.[24]

In these writers we have an account of intentional engagement in which a subject shows understanding of her world via bodily engagements made intelligible by perceptual experiences, whose contents already contain the possibilities of such engagement. The rationality of such responses is not a consequence of their being the outcome of sequences of reasoning conforming to objective standards. It is anchored in the way the world is experienced by the subject, a grasp of which is required if the appropriateness of the response is to become manifest. Rationality has become immanent to that situation. Within this account rationality has become equated to a certain kind of intelligibility or appropriateness of response in the context of the way the world appears. (Hence the distinction between emotional and rational responses to the world is undermined. For both can seem intelligible given the way the world appears to a subject. Nonetheless there is a difference between expressive and intentional bodily responses. Our imagined world, as we have discussed in previous chapters, is a world of affect. The affective content is mapped by our expressive responses. For intentional engagement, however, we need not only recognition of acts as desirable/ undesirable but also as possible, as something we can do. The comportment towards the world in intentional engagement is *projective*, we are directing our behaviour towards a goal which, as Sartre emphasises, is *not* currently the case.)

Bildung, Habitus and Performativity

The anchorage of rational intelligibility within the situated world of the subject does not render it an individual or personal matter. For Heidegger understanding of the kind he outlined was a shared practice: 'the world is always already primarily given as the common world',[25] one into which we are initiated as we grow up within a culture. Merleau-Ponty also insists that the world of the subject is a world with others. For both writers the general background in the context of which certain possibilities make sense includes the cultural anchorage of embodied subjects. For Wittgenstein the appropriateness of a practice depended on it being a shared one. It is incoherent to imagine a rule into the following of which others could not be initiated. Such behaviour could not be seen as reflecting 'a grasp on things' at all. If the practice is to yield a possible way in which the world appears, then such an appearance, albeit contextual, must in principle be available to others. Within German philosophy the process of orientation to a world which is salient to us, a world thereby taking on a form for engagement, is captured by the term *Bildung*.[26] The history of this concept is discussed by Gadamer at the beginning of his major work *Truth and Method*, in which he emphasises its historical nature. What is suggested by this concept is the 'historical constitution of man',[27] in which 'that by which and through which one is formed becomes completely one's own'.[28]

On Gadamer's own account all experiences and judgements involve *prejudices*, prejudgements, without which they would not be possible. Such prejudices determine our *horizons*, what we can see of the world from our particular standpoints within it. We are not aware of them as such. Rather 'there is always a world, already interpreted, into which our experience slips'.[29] The passing on of such prejudices is, for Gadamer, primarily through the vehicle of language. John McDowell also gives a picture which is close to that of Gadamer:

> Initiation into conceptual capacities, which includes responsiveness ... to rational demands ... is a normal part of what it is for a human being to come to maturity. The resulting habits of thought and action are second nature ... it is what features in German philosophy as *Bildung*.[30]

For Gadamer and McDowell the initation into culture was primarily through the initiation into language. Other writers, however, emphasise the bodily nature of such a process and it is to these that we now turn. Pierre Bourdieu does this with his key notion of the *habitus*. In common with both Heidegger and Merleau-Ponty, Bourdieu opposed an intellectualist account of human agency. Such accounts, he claims, are guilty of 'substituting the observer's relation to a practice for the practical relation to practice'.[31] He was equally dismissive of accounts which saw actions as a species of mechanical causation or, in contrast, as the outcome of pure acts of will. Our habitual engagements with the world are ones which 'neither the extrinsic and instantaneous determinisms of a mechanical sociologism nor the purely internal but equally punctual determination of voluntarist or spontaneous subjectivism are capable of accounting for'.[32] Bourdieu felt, however, that the phenomenological tradition had not paid sufficient attention to material and social structures as the context within which constituting practices took place. He introduced his key term habitus as a way of bringing together social institutions and the experiences and practices of the agents who make them up. For Bourdieu the habitus is, in his much repeated phrase, 'a system of durable, transposable dispositions'. These function as the 'generative basis of structured, objectively unified practices'.[33] These practices are 'regular, without being the product of obedience to rules, objectively adapted to their goals without presupposing a conscious aiming at ends'.[34] These dispositions are a reflection of the social and material features of a particular environment in which individuals are placed, for example, the class structure or the power relations between men and women. There is some kind of relation of 'fit' between the habitus and the social structures, and the habitus varies with distinct social positions. Social structures are viewed as productive of the habitus.

The sets of behaviour which are thereby engendered also work to maintain the social institutions in place. Individuals who share a social position will share a habitus, though, as no one's social history is exactly identical to that of another, this is more a case of 'homology, of diversity within homogeneity'.[35] For Bourdieu, the habitus is learnt through imitation,

> practical mastery is transmitted in practice ... Body *hexis* speaks directly to the motor function ... children are particularly attentive to the gestures and postures ... a way of walking, a tilt of the head, facial expressions, ways of sitting and using implements ... bodily *hexis* is a political mythology realised, *em-bodied*, turned into a permanent disposition, a durable manner of standing, speaking.[36]

Children are therefore initiated into culture, learn to occupy their appropriate places by such bodily imitations, so that the structures of the society are maintained 'through injunctions as insignificant as "sit up straight" or "don't hold your knife in your left hand"'.[37] In this way the body retains the traces of its own history, which in its habitual responses, or practical sense (*sens practique*), have become incorporated as a 'second nature'. For Bourdieu the speaking of a language, rather than forming the basis of all cultural initiation, is itself an example of one such habitus. The rules or norms required are implicit within practices of speaking which are learnt mimetically.

> All symbolic domination presupposes, on the part of those who submit to it, a form of complicity which is neither passive submission to external constraint nor a free adherence to values. The recognition of the legitimacy of the official language has nothing in common with explicitly professed, deliberate and revocable belief, or with the intentional act of accepting a norm.[38]

Ordinary language incorporates not only linguistic norms for Bourdieu but also social and political ones. It is moulded by social relations of power in ways which are not usually transparent. Such moulding forms our perceptions of our world, the actions and beliefs we find intelligible, and thereby helps to maintain the status quo.

Thus far Bourdieu is providing a powerful description of the way in which the social becomes bodily reproduced. What is less clear is how this account separates itself from the social determinism, which he explicitly rejects. What becomes clear, however, is that the inculcation of a habitus is not simply a question of mechanical learning. We not only pick up behaviour, but thereby pick up its *rationale*. In acting the agent is aware that there is a difference between a right and wrong way of proceeding, even though this may not find articulation beyond that of it *feeling* right or wrong. There is an implicit sense of conforming to norms. What this makes clear is that the habitus, though learnt through bodily imitations, is more than a learnt disposition to behave in a certain way in certain objectively specifiable situations. It is rather a 'matrix of perceptions, apperceptions and actions'.[39] It provides a schema for making sense of the world, and for recognising certain responses as reasonable or unreasonable in the light of it. By such bodily imitations the child grasps a whole way of experiencing the world. 'The body believes in what it plays at: it weeps if it mimes grief'.[40] What the child is grasping is a certain way of seeing the world which make certain actions show up as possible, some as unthinkable etc. Practical evaluation of a situation is then governed by 'a whole body of wisdom, sayings, commonplaces, ethical precepts ("that's not for the likes of us")'.[41] The child's relation to her action therefore is not one of blind compliance, the actions make sense to her . They give the social world a 'physiognomy'. The link of such a matrix of perception and action to social positioning, however, has the consequence that

> habitus which have been produced by different modes of generation, that is by conditions of existence which, in imposing different definitions of the impossible, the possible, and the probable, cause one group to experience as natural or reasonable practices which another group find unthinkable or scandalous, and vice versa.[42]

The overall picture is then one of the 'appropriating by the world of a body, thus enabled to appropriate the world'.[43] Here, as noted by other writers, we might be reminded of Pascal. One kneels in prayer and only later acquires belief. In this context, however, the kneeling yields the belief, as that which makes the kneeling itself intelligible.

In a theory, which, like Bourdieu, gives an account of the way in which the social is embodied, or made corporeal, Judith Butler employs poststructuralist rather than phenomenological or Marxist sources. In her theory of *performativity* Butler offers an account of the way in which social norms become incorporated as bodily practices, with many parallels to that offered by Bourdieu. Social norms become bodily by the reproduction of both linguistic and non-linguistic bodily acts. These acts, as for Bourdieu, are not mechanical responses, but carry meaning and significance. Both the subject, and interdependently the world, become formed by them. What is said and done does not reflect the inner processes of an already constituted subject, receiving information concerning an independently structured world. This is, of course, the intellectualist picture. Rather the saying and the doing are productive of both the subject and world. It is via initiation into bodily practices, via the imitation and repetition of bodily acts, that the world, and interdependently the subject, takes shape. Butler's primary focus of concern has been the production of sex and gender differences by means of such bodily performances. When the baby is born the midwife pronounces 'it's a girl', and wraps her in pink. This is followed by a set of differential practices, including later those of the child itself, which collectively structure the world into male and female and serve to make intelligible differential responses in the light of such structuring.

These performances give a meaning or form to these institutions which make the practices which maintain them seem justified, often natural and inevitable. The extent to which the institutions are constituted by such performances remains invisible, for instead they appear part of the world of nature. Here Butler moves beyond the conception of nature, which had informed certain writers making use of the concept of *Bildung*. For them *Bildung* was the process by which nature turned itself into culture, it nonetheless being an integral part of nature to be susceptible to such a process. This is also the picture offered us by McDowell. For Butler, however, it becomes clear that what counts as nature for us is itself produced by our performative acts.

Parallel as Bourdieu's and Butler's accounts are in many respects, there are, however, some key differences, which reveal the differing frameworks within which they are located. Bourdieu follows in the tradition of Heidegger and Merleau-Ponty in viewing the bodily practices towards the world as yielding a world for a subject. The subjectivity of such a subject is constituted out of the way the world appears to them. This may not be articulable ('that's not for the likes of us'), but the interdependence of the appearance of the world and the responses to it are what make such responses, for the subject, intelligible and appropriate. They are what the world, experienced in a certain way, seems to require. The rationality is immanent within the experience itself, while nonetheless resulting from the incorporation of social norms. Indeed the power of such norms comes, for Bourdieu, from their formative role in the constitution of such appearances. The habitus is thus a generative matrix, generating perceptions and appearances of the world as well as possible responses to it.

Butler, however, along with other poststructuralist writers, has no room for the concept of experience, which for her suggests a domain of the inner, hidden from public view, serving to constitute the subject, and act as a guarantor to meaning and a foundation to knowledge. For Butler the meaning and significance which bodily practices carry is not a matter of the way the world appears to subjects at specific locations within it, an appearance which makes intelligible their responses. Rather the significance is an effect of the practices in context, and as such a matter of public negotiation. What is lost is what Merleau-Ponty refers to as 'the consciousness' or sometimes the 'experience of rationality'.[44] The normativity which marks intentional engagement becomes simply a matter of incorporating social norms. What marks Butler's account here is a kind of externalism, a feature which it shares with the intellectualist tradition, which it otherwise repudiates. This feature may not be immediately obvious. First, one of the main directions of Butler's concern is the formation of the subject. The subject becomes constituted performatively, by its bodily acts and those of others towards it, which produce it as male or female, working class or not etc. This account of the production of the subject, however, does not seem an adequate account of the production of subjectivity. Butler does, of course, talk of 'the bodily *doxa*', as 'lived and corporeally registered sets of beliefs that constitute social reality'.[45] These beliefs, however, which constitute the world of the subject, are given by bodily performances, which carry with them a meaning and significance ascertainable from a third person point of view. They are not perspectival. They do not require engagement with the subject's point of view to be grasped. The rationality or appropriateness of these performances is then not a matter of their relation to the world as experienced by the subject. They count as rational if they conform to social norms, they count as irrational if they are outside of them. Here we have lost the sense of our engagement with the world as manifesting understanding in Heidegger's sense, and the corresponding possibility of our finding our own actions and those of others intelligible in a way that outruns a simple recognition of conformity. (The issue of whether an account of subjectivity, which sees it as constituted from the meaning of acts interpreted from a third personal perspective, is satisfactory is further discussed in the following chapter.)

Tradition, Determinacy and Change

Nonetheless there is a danger of the sound of jackboots marching in an account of reason and agency which has its roots in notions of tradition, *Bildung* or related concepts. We are initiated into a community with whom we learn to march in step, and the coincidence in our steps constitutes our mutual intelligibility. My ordinary activities are just part of a web of social activities in which people unreflectively participate, without opposing what they are doing to what others do. My acts are intelligible to myself and others only because others are acting appropriately and in a regular fashion. This picture, however, can suggest too great a homogeneity within communities, and too static a conception of the meanings which our worlds hold for us. (It also makes it difficult to see a role for rational reflection, and makes it difficult to see how understanding and assessment could take place in relation to those occupying different communities. We will address these questions in the following section.)

In this context Butler criticises Bourdieu for an overly static and determinist conception of the meaning yielded by our bodily responses to the world. In this critique Butler is brokering a dispute, which she sees between the work of Bourdieu and that of Derrida. For Bourdieu the habitus is the consequence of particular social positioning and, in the context of that positioning, yields a determinate sense and intelligibility both to the world and the agents' practices. Where context changes there will be a 'lack of fit', between the habitus and the objective conditions and eventually a new habitus will emerge. As we saw above, given that the social conditions only produce appropriate practices through yielding for the subject a meaningful world, there is, for Bourdieu, some degree of openness in both the significance conferred and the corresponding practices. However, whatever these practices are, they result in an objective regularity which collectively maintains the institutions which bring them into being.

Derrida, in contrast, rather than emphasising the *sedimentation* of meaning in social acts, pays attention to the 'break' which occurs between one context of utterance and the next. For Derrida, and as we shall see for Butler, the temporal dimensions to meaning are central to it. The meaning of a word is dependent on a temporal history of usages. Whenever we use a term we are engaged in an act of citation. We are repeating a word, echoing its previous usages. This repeatability, termed *iterability*, does not always produce stability of meaning. For each new repetition is in a different situation, which effects a *break* from the past use which is echoed. The effect on meaning of the new situation is not that of simply reproducing past signification. The meaning of utterances and other social acts remains thereby unpredictable and radically indeterminate. Bourdieu criticises Derrida for an inability to account for stability and communicability of meaning within cultural contexts and for providing no account of the social conditions within which meaning is produced. Derrida's insistence on the break makes it a structural feature of all language use and thereby abstracts from links to particular social conditions.[46]

In brokering this dispute Butler agrees with Bourdieu that Derrida's insistence on the break as a general feature of language use does not enable attention to the social contexts within which meaning arises, 'paralysing the social analysis of forceful utterance'.[47] Neither does it accommodate the sedimentation of meaning within corporeal practices, the history of bodies made present, the way that social norms are made into second nature, 'configuring and restricting the *doxa* that counts as "reality"'.[48] 'The "constructive" power of the tacit performative is precisely its ability to establish a practical sense for the body, not only a sense of what the body is, but how it can or cannot negotiate space, its "location" in terms of prevailing cultural coordinates.'[49] Nonetheless Butler is critical of Bourdieu for amplifying 'the social dimension of the performative at the expense of its transformability'.[50] 'Bourdieu fails to take account of the way in which a performative can break with existing context and assume new contexts',[51] thereby refiguring the terms of legitimacy. Her attention to the temporal dimension of meaning, its iterability, leaves space for an openness of signification and its corresponding justificatory relations, which allow for an indeterminacy in meaning and appropriate responses, even within what might be viewed as a continuing tradition.

For Bourdieu the emergence of a new habitus comes when social conditions change so that existing practices no longer fit. There are two aspects to this. They both no longer make sense and no longer yield the objective patterns which are required by the social field. (It is unclear in Bourdieu how these two aspects are related.) For Butler things are less orderly. The feature of iterability leaves open the possibility of meanings emerging in ways which are not predictable. This is partly a consequence of the bodily nature of the meaning-conveying practices. The body itself is *excessive*, it outruns any meaning which can be attached to it. Consequently any bodily practices are open to the possibility of resignification, of being taken in different ways, at different times. 'The body rhetorically exceeds the … act it also performs. This excess is what Bourdieu's account appears to miss, or, perhaps to suppress.'[52] 'Bodies are formed by social norms, but the process of that formation runs its risks. Thus the situation of constrained contingency that governs the discursive and social formation of the body and its (re)productions remains unacknowledged by Bourdieu.'[53] The fact of such iterability is what, for Butler, stops us being trapped within the framework of signification, which for Bourdieu fits our social situation.

(Two men appear to get married. They wear white suits and sport flower bouquets. The uttering of the marriage vows in a context which the social field renders illegitimate has the consequence, on Bourdieu's account, of the act remaining unintelligible. It fails to be an instance of the practice of marrying. For Butler the act opens up the possibility of resignifying familial relations to render the act meaningful, though contrary to dominant social norms.)

Immanent Rationality and Negotiating Difference

In the accounts discussed above rationality is both immanent and perspectival. The intelligibility of our beliefs about the world and our responses to it resides in the meaning and significance which the world has for us, itself a consequence of our comportment towards it. If we follow Bourdieu the significance the world has for us rests on social practices into which we are initiated. Intentional engagement is bodily engagement made intelligible by the appearance of the subject's world.

On such an account intelligibility and rationality appear to be conflated. We need to consider, however, whether the intelligibility of certain responses guarantees their rationality? Does the intelligibility of an act ensure we have some reason to perform it, or, more demandingly, a good reason? If intelligibility and rationality are conflated then, on finding her anger intelligible, we find that the subject had a reason to shout. What space is there then for the thought that it would nonetheless have been better if she had not done so? The space here for reflective deliberation seems unclear. How does such a picture accommodate the critical rational scrutiny of beliefs and behaviour by laying bare their basis, an activity which for many philosophers has constituted the sphere of reason? Can we accommodate the frustrations of a child being initiated into a habitus in which 'girls don't do that kind of thing', if we do not have available to us the move that this view is irrational, for no good reasons can be given for it, or none that bear scrutiny once spelt out? The extent to which reason has become immanent here seems to render it problematic as a tool of such scrutiny.

The issue, which is being raised here, is not one simply concerning the presence or absence of linguistic articulation. As we discussed above language can be used in our everyday practical engagement with our world. Its use, however, does not necessarily lead to reflectivity, if only because, as Bourdieu pointed out, language use itself is a habitus. If language is not sufficient for reflectivity neither does it seem necessary for it. We can hesitate over our acts, wondering if our stitches in a piece of sewing look right, for example, without being able to articulate this process. The possibility for reflection on the rationality of our acts suggests stepping back from habitual engagement, and subjecting it to scrutiny. On most accounts such reflection requires us to abandon perspectivity and invoke some standards of transcendent reason.

In Bourdieu's account of the habitus he invokes a relation of 'fit' between the habitus and the social field. In one sense, as we discussed above, this is an objectivist notion in which the practices the habitus engender objectively reinforce the social institutions concerned. In another sense, however, the considerations of fit have a hermeneutic reading. The scheme of perception generated must make sense of the subject's environment. '[Habitus] is an open set of dispositions that is constantly subjected to experiences, and therefore constantly affected by them in a way that either reinforces or modifies its structures'.[54] Articulating such a notion of fit is a difficult task. We cannot stand outside our frameworks of meaning and see whether or not they fit. This is a judgement which we have to make within our perspective. Reflection is provoked by an unease, a sense of things not quite hanging together. In many of our everyday acts and judgements the unease which might prompt reflection does not arise, and the constructedness of our schemas for making sense of the world does not come into view. There are, however, a number of things which might bring this into view and prompt reflection on the most satisfactory way of seeing the world. First, as we have discussed previously, the world of our experience is an imaginary world. it is structured not just by possibilities but by affect. The images in terms of which we make sense of our world reflect social imaginaries, but are not exhausted by them. The imaginary structure of our world also reflects personal histories of bodily encounters and relations with significant others, which may form a basis of resistance to the social imaginaries into which we are initiated by culture. The affective content of our imaginary world acts as a drag on the social significance that world can take on, acting as a resistance to the social meanings into which we are being initiated. (Take, for example, the social significance of the term 'mother', which can be undermined by personal histories of conflict or neglect.) The imaginary dimension of our experiences of the world thereby blocks both social determinism of the kind Bourdieu is accused of and the reduction of the psyche to the social, which can be seen as a problem in Butler's work.

The second feature which can prompt reflectivity is the fact that we occupy many different social locations, each of which can generate a particular habitus, not all of which can be simultaneously livable. We are therefore required to negotiate the differences between them. Thirdly, there are encounters with others who experience the world differently, which throws into relief the possibility of alternatives, unsettling the 'second nature' which our own frameworks have come to occupy. All of these require negotiation of difference in signification, by reflection concerning which way to make sense of our world.

The philosopher who most famously describes the encounter with difference is Gadamer. Gadamer is concerned with what understanding consists in. 'It is not based', he says, 'in transposing oneself into another person', rather it is 'to come to an understanding about the subject matter, not to get inside another person and relive his experience'.[55] As discussed above, for Gadamer, all experiences and judgements involve *prejudices*. However, our prejudices do not form frameworks of understanding which are like closed boxes. They provide openings whereby new and different interpretations of the world can be encountered. In this encounter it is not the case that we simply leave our prejudices and adopt those of others. Neither do we simply engage our prejudices in making sense of theirs. Rather the encounter serves to make evident the prejudices informing our accounts of the world which previously had appeared as transparent reflections of the world in itself. It also opens up the possibility of seeing the world differently, if we can engage sufficiently with the forms of life of others to recognise the possibility of experiencing the world in the way they do. This process is essentially dialogic, an ongoing conversation in which understanding consists in a *fusion of horizons*, a fusion which emerges out of the encounter and is not restricted to adopting either of the perspectives within it.

What is clear from Gadamer's work is that this process is a process of rational assessment. The modification of experience here is not a brutely causal matter. It is a recognition of alternative rational demands. It is an assessment that certain ways of seeing can make sense. Nonetheless it is not a process which results from adopting an Archimedean standpoint outside prejudgements. It does, however, rest on the assumption that we are living together in a shared world and in some sense our common humanity makes possible such encounters. To understand the perspective of another requires engaging with the way our shared world appears from another (interpretive) location. As we have seen, the way the world appears is tied up with whole sets of practices and ways of life. To assess such appearances requires entering sufficiently into a way of life to recognise or dissent from the appropriateness of certain ways of characterising the world. There are limits to all our capacities for such understanding, which always remain partial. What is central, however, is the recognition that a different viewpoint has an impact on our own.

The difficulty here comes in recognising such encounters as processes of rational engagement, in the absence of agreed criteria or procedures of evaluation, with respect to which differing views can be assessed. The picture outlined does not dispense with the use of such agreed criteria. Within specific communities, such as scientific communities sharing certain paradigms of interpretation, such criteria play a central role in daily practices of evaluation. Their application, however, is still a matter of a learned practice, and the possibility of more radical challenge, resting on 'seeing' the data in a different way, remains always in play.

Jürgen Habermas in many ways follows Gadamer's intersubjective account of understanding. He maintains that we must

> give up the paradigm of the philosophy of consciousness – namely a subject that represents objects and toils with them – in favour of the paradigm of ... intersubjective understanding and communication ... and put the cognitive-instrumental aspect of reason in its place as part of a more encompassing communicative rationality.[56]

Nonetheless he was critical of Gadamer's account for what he sees as its inadequacies in recognising the power relations, which shape the traditions and conventions that condition our understanding. Habermas lays down conditions for an *ideal speech situation* within which rational negotiation across difference would be possible, a situation in which no participants can distort the process by exploiting their superior power in a way that deprives others of a voice in determining the outcome. In so far as actual speech situations fail to conform to such an ideal Habermas thought we could scrutinise the prejudgements or prejudices they involve to arrive, on analogy with psychoanalysis, at a depth interpretation which will unmask ideological presuppositions. This is the nub of the disagreement between him and Gadamer. For Gadamer insists there is no position from which such a depth interpretation can be made, for indeed there is no position which abstracts from the specific historical context of dialogue. There is therefore no transcendent position from which the conditions for ideal communication can be articulated.

In a move, which in many ways parallels that of Habermas, Bourdieu gives the position of reflective scrutiny to the social scientist. While we unthinkingly occupy our habitus in our everyday engagement with the world, the social scientist can see the way in which such a habitus has been produced, and map its relation to social power, and consequently reflect on the advantages and disadvantages of continuing with it. Such an account seems problematic in the same way as that of Habermas. In privileging the position of the social scientist Bourdieu is in danger of portraying the significance which practices have to their practitioners as in some way illusory.[57] Moreover Bourdieu's own work shows that you cannot step outside a habitus, even if you recognise that you have one. It is not therefore clear what the position is, which would allow such detached study.[58] What would rather seem to follow from his account is that the methods and reflections of the social scientists themselves constitute a habitus, rather than some transcendent position from which the habitus can be assessed.

A debate of rather a different kind is found in Gadamer's encounter with Derrida.[59] Gadamer opens up space for reflection, and confronts the apparent spectre of different rationalities, by invoking the possibilities of reflective understanding across difference. Gadamer's optimism about the possibility of mutual understanding, of 'completely understanding the other's meaning', is brought into question by Derrida. Derrida sees this as requiring a determinacy of meaning, which, as we have seen above, his own work throws into question. It would also be to ignore the 'necessary moment of distance, interruption', which necessarily marks any mediation, what for Derrida constitutes *the otherness of the other*. (This we shall discuss further in the following chapter.) As David Wood comments: 'in the very process of grasping what the other is saying, at the very point of understanding, we must take a step back, allow the movement of assimilation to be interrupted'.[60] However, as Wood points out in his discussion of this encounter, Gadamer himself seems to make space for the kind of considerations which Derrida brings to the fore. 'Between two people this [mutual agreement] … would require a never ending dialogue.' Moreover, the never-ending dialogue is 'for essential reasons'; 'there is a potentiality for being other that lies beyond every coming to agreement about what is common'.[61] Consequently, the experiences, which Gadamer refers to, of finding ourselves perfectly understood are always open to the possibility of future developments, which undermine such confidence. Gadamer himself understood that horizons of understanding were not insulated one from the other. The experience of the disruption of mutual intelligibility which remains in play in any dialogic encounter (whether within or across selves) marks the moment of difference from which prejudices come into view and reflection on the possibility of orientating oneself to the world in a different way becomes opened up. Here the difference between Derrida and Gadamer seems to rest on the degree of optimism with which they regard the possibility of mutual agreement following from such moments of disruption. In maintaining optimism, however, Gadamer seems committed to an openness in our relations to others, which does not allow appropriative understanding of their difference within our own framework, any more than it suggests an abandonment of our own positionality to lose ourselves in theirs. Both possibilities he explicitly rejects.

Despite the ability of Gadamer's account to accommodate aspects of Derrida's critique there remain some important differences. Derrida's suspicions require an ongoing vigilance for those working within the hermeneutic framework. For Gadamer complete agreement is an unrealisable ideal informing our practice. For Derrida adoption of such an ideal involves, as Wood comments, 'the permanent lure of deepening', a failure to recognise the necessary incompleteness of understanding in the face of 'an excess which cannot be completely accomodated'.[62] Such an excess ensures, as we discussed above, that the repetitions of utterances or bodily acts which are taken to mark mutual agreement, are subject to an iterability which belies their apparent determinacy.

Taking on board such vigilance, however, need not undermine the insistence on an *implicit publicness*, which informs the approach to rationality and understanding of the writers we have been discussing in this chapter. If our intentional engagements are to manifest, in some sense, a grasp of a shared world, to which they constitute an intelligible response, then such a grasp must be available to others. It must be one which others could be initiated into, via practices of linguistic or other bodily imitation. This can be recognised together with the fact that the process of imitation, for example, by gay couples of heterosexual marriage, can extend the range of what we find intelligible.

The paradigm of rational reflection which is being invoked here is very different from the sequences of propositions which are commonly held up as examples of the giving of reasons. They rule out the child's dismissal of her family's prejudices as irrational on the grounds that they cannot give reasons for them beyond 'that's not the kind of things girls do'. The irrationality of the belief, if it is to be shown, has to rest on different methods. It requires grasping the way the family experiences the world, and recognising that this is a 'possible' way of seeing things, given the range of experiences they have. (Note, this is a quite different process from the sociological claim that people of this generation from this social milieu generally hold views like that.) The way to unsettle the belief is to expose the possibility of different scenarios which modify the experiences, provide a different way of seeing the world, and thereby yield different normative claims.

Summary

In this chapter we have attempted to replace an account of intentional engagement with the world in terms of the availability of practical reasoning with an account anchored in 'understanding', in the Heideggerian sense. Intentional acts are bodily responses to a world experienced as making them appropriate. The rationality required of such acts is perspectival and available to those who can grasp how the world appears to subjects within it. Such perspectivity, however, does not make the rationality of our responses a *private* matter. Our modes of experiencing our world are ones into which we are socially and culturally initiated, in part by the moulding of our bodily responses.

Consequently claims of rationality are subject to constraints of an implicit publicness.

The immanence of such an account of rationality raises issues of conservatism, difference and reflection. We have suggested that such issues can be addressed employing resources from both hermeneutics and poststructuralism. Gadamer's account of the fusion of horizons needs to be informed by Derrida's vigilance in respect of the otherness of the other and the pervasiveness of iterability. What emerges is a picture of subjects negotiating a shared world from differing positions within it.

Notes

1. For the concept of *Bildung* see note 26.
2. John McDowell uses the idea of second nature in *Mind and World* (Cambridge, MA: Harvard University Press, 1994).
3. D. Davidson, 'Actions, Reasons and Causes', in D. Davidson, *Essays on Actions and Events* (Oxford: Clarendon Press, 1980).
4. See for example J. A. Fodor, *The Language of Thought* (New York: Thomas Crowell, 1975).
5. See D. Davidson, 'Radical Interpretation', in D. Davidson, *Inquiries into Truth and Interpretation* (Oxford: Clarendon Press, 1984); and D. C. Dennett, *The Intentional Stance* (Cambridge, MA: Bradford Books/MIT Press, 1987).
6. J. McDowell, 'Functionalism and Anomalous Monism', in E. Lepore and B. McLaughlin (eds), *Actions and Events: Perspectives on to the Philosophy of Donald Davidson* (Oxford: Blackwell, 1985).
7. J. Searle, 'Consciousness, Intentionality and the Background', in J. Searle, *The Rediscovery of the Mind* (Cambridge, MA: MIT Press, 1992).
8. See L. Wittgenstein, *Philosophical Investigations* (Oxford: Blackwell, 1958).
9. C. Taylor, 'To Follow a Rule ... ', in M. Postone, E. LiPuma and C. Calhoun (eds), *Bourdieu: Critical Perspectives* (Cambridge: Polity Press, 1983).
10. Ibid., p. 47.
11. Ibid., p. 48.
12. McDowell, *Mind and World*, Lecture 1.
13. McDowell, 'Functionalism and Anomalous Monism', p. 396.
14. There are, however, crucial differences between McDowell and Heidegger here, as McDowell continues to think of the exercise of spontaneity within an intellectualist model, into which experience feeds conceptualised premisses. For Heidegger the possibility of reasoning of that kind requires a pre-reflective engagement with a world already salient to us.
15. M. Heidegger, *Being and Time*, trans. J. Maquarrie and E. Robinson (Oxford: Blackwell, 1967), H 336.
16. Ibid., p. 145.
17. H. L. Dreyfus, *Being-in-the-World: A Commentary on Heidegger's Being and Time, Division 1* (Cambridge, MA: MIT Press, 1991), p. 190.
18. M. Merleau-Ponty, *Phenomenology of Perception*, trans. C. Smith (London: Routledge, 1962), p. 137.

19. Ibid., pp. 129–30.
20. Ibid., p. 139.
21. Ibid., p. 143.
22. Ibid., p. 110. This patient is contrasted to the patient we referred to in Chapter 1, who was capable of concrete but not abstract movements.
23. P. Ricoeur, 'Imagination in Discourse and in Action', in G. Robinson and J. Rundell (eds), *Rethinking Imagination, Culture and Creativity* (London: Routledge, 1994), p. 126.
24. J. N. Mohanty, *The Self and Its Other* (New Delhi: Oxford University Press, 2000), pp. 130–1.
25. Quoted Dreyfus, *Being-in-the-World*, p. 154.
26. For a discussion of the origins of this concept see R. Bubner, 'Bildung and Second Nature', in N. Smith (ed.), *Reading McDowell on Mind and World* (London: Routledge, 2002).
27. H. G. Gadamer, *Truth and Method*, 2nd edn (London: Sheed and Ward, 1989), p. 15.
28. Ibid., p. 11.
29. See H. G. Gadamer, *Philosophical Hermeneutics*, trans. and ed. D. E. Linge (Berkeley, CA: University of California Press, 1977); extracts reprinted in R. Kearney and M. Rainwater (eds), *The Continental Philosophy Reader* (London: Routledge, 1996), p. 120.
30. McDowell, *Mind and World*, p. 84.
31. C. Taylor, 'To Follow a Rule ... ', p. 55.
32. P. Bourdieu, *Outline of a Theory of Practice*, trans. R. Nice (Cambridge: Cambridge University Press, 1977), p. 82.
33. H. Dreyfus and P. Rabinow, 'Can There Be a Science of Existential Structure and Social Meaning?', in Postone, LiPuma and Calhoun (eds), *Bourdieu*.
34. Bourdieu, *Outline of a Theory of Practice*, p. 72.
35. Ibid., p. 86.
36. P. Bourdieu, *The Logic of Practice* (Cambridge: Polity Press, 1990), p. 87.
37. Taylor, 'To Follow a Rule ... ', p. 58.
38. P. Bourdieu, *Language and Symbolic Power* (Cambridge: Polity Press, 1991), pp. 50–5, p. 55.
39. Bourdieu, *Logic of Practice*, p. 83.
40. L. McNay, *Gender and Agency* (Cambridge: Polity, 2000), p. 39.
41. Bourdieu, *Logic of Practice*, p. 77.
42. Ibid., p. 78.
43. Ibid., p. 89.
44. M. Merleau-Ponty, *The Primacy of Perception*, ed. J. Edie (Evanson, IL: Northwestern University Press, 1964), p. 25.
45. J. Butler, *Excitable Speech: A Politics of the Performative* (New York and London: Routledge, 1997), p. 159.
46. J. Derrida, *Writing and Difference*, trans. A. Bass (London: Routledge and Kegan Paul, 1978).
47. Butler, *Excitable Speech*, p. 150.
48. Ibid., p. 159.
49. Ibid., pp. 159–60.
50. Ibid., p. 151.
51. Ibid., p. 150.

52. Ibid., p. 155.
53. Ibid., p. 156.
54. P. Bourdieu, *An Invitation to Reflexive Sociology* (Cambridge: Polity Press, 1992), p. 133.
55. Gadamer, *Truth and Method*, p. 76.
56. J. Habermas, *The Theory of Communicative Action* (London: Heinemann, 1984), vol. 1, p. 390.
57. See the discussion in Dreyfus and Rabinow, 'Can There Be a Science ... ?'
58. Ibid.
59. For a discussion of the (absence of) encounter between Gadamer and Derrida see D. Wood, 'Vigilance and Interruption: Derrida, Gadamer and the Limits of Dialogue', in D. Wood, *Philosophy at the Limit* (London: Unwin, 1990). We are grateful to Lawrence Nixon for bringing this chapter to our attention.
60. Ibid., p. 127.
61. Ibid.
62. Ibid., p. 128.

7

Ourselves and Others

Mutually Constituting Subjectivities

In previous chapters we have offered an account of subjectivity in terms of an embodied perspective onto a world of objects. These intentional objects of consciousness are themselves mutually constituted by the perspectives of subjects so that the world and the subject are inter-dependent. The subjectivity involved here is expressed in a body whose comportment towards the world maps the shape the world takes for the subject and thereby maps the content of such subjectivity itself.

In this chapter the focus of our attention will shift to the role played in the constitution of subjectivity by other subjects. Here a distinction needs to be made between *general and particular others*. We have drawn attention in most of our discussions thus far to the role of the social (generalised others), in the formation of our ways of experiencing our world. We are initiated into our way of experiencing a world by our initiation into a culture, with a perspective onto a shared world along-side other subjects. For Heidegger, for example, the 'self of everyday Dasein is the *they-self* ... the particular Dasein has been *dispersed* into the "they" ... this characterises the kind of Being which we know as concernful absorption in the world we encounter as closest to us'.[1] Here the 'they' into which 'we' are absorbed has a certain anonymity, 'those from whom, for the most part, one does *not* distinguish oneself – those among whom one is too'.[2] Our ordinary activities are just part of a web of social activities in which people unreflectively participate, without opposing what they are doing to what others do. Central as such accounts are in resisting a picture of a subject whose experiences are formed in isolation (of which more below), they are in danger of reducing the psyche to the social. We also need an account of *individual* subjectivities. For Heidegger such an account was provided without reference to others. For what supposedly raises *Dasein* from its absorption in the social world is none other than its realisation that it must face its own death, that its life is, in this sense, its own alone, not sharable by anyone else. It is through such realisation that *Dasein* achieves an 'authentic' existence, in which 'one' is individuated from the 'they' and assumes responsibility for one's actions. We will not be pursuing these claims here, except to comment that within them notions of authenticity and responsibility are desocialised in a doubtfully intelligible way. Rather we will be resisting the absorption of the 'I' into the 'they' from two directions. One pays attention to the role played by *particular* others in the formation of subjectivity. This emphasis is found in both psychoanalytic and phenomenological work. The second direction we shall explore pays attention to radical alterity, or difference, as a dimension of our relations to others. This is found, for example in the work of Levinas and Derrida.

Epistemological Dilemmas

In Virginia Woolf's novel *To the Lighthouse* a young woman, Lily, wants to understand the older woman, Mrs. Ramsey, whom she so much admires.

> She imagined how in the chambers of the mind and heart of the woman who was physically touching her, were stood, like the treasures in the tombs of kings, tablets bearing sacred inscriptions, which, if one could spell them out would teach one everything, but they would never be offered openly, never made public ... [3]

Lily's problem in coming to understand Mrs. Ramsey is, in part, a practical one: Mrs. Ramsey is elusive and incommunicative. But the problem is also philosophical. For Lily starts off from a picture of the mind of another that makes it difficult to see how such understanding could ever be gained. Here the picture seems to be the classic Cartesian one of the mind as a secret realm, known only to its owner. Our only access then seems to be by some assumed analogy to ourselves and, where we feel such an analogy fails, the inner realm of others remains a mystery. In dominant Anglo-American philosophy of mind such a picture has given way to one in which psychological states are inner mechanisms which produce behaviour. We grasp these mechanisms by application of folk psychology, a theory we apply to others and thereby make hypotheses about the kind of inner states which could be producing their external behaviour. In a more recent variant we simulate their state and, assuming we share psychological mechanisms, predict and explain their behaviour on the basis of our simulation. In each case the goal is knowledge of inner workings.

This epistemological dilemma and its consequent responses are criticised by Merleau-Ponty, when discussing the relation of ourselves and others in *The Primacy of Perception*. He points out how early children are sensitive and responsive to facial expressions, for example, a smile.

> How could that be possible if, in order to arrive at an understanding of the global meaning of the smile and to learn that the smile is a fair indication of a benevolent feeling, the child had to perform [such a] complicated task ... beginning with the visual perception of another's smile, he had to compare that visual perception of the smile with the movements that he himself makes when he is happy or when he feels benevolent – projecting to the other a benevolence of which he would have had intimate experience but which could not be grasped directly in the other.[4]

Apart from the complexity of the intellectual reasoning required in either the argument from analogy, the application of a folk theory or the use of simulation, there are other problems with this approach. It assumes that the child has some knowledge of the bodily movements he makes, which can then be compared to those made by the subject he is observing, constructing a point-by-point correspondence between the visual image of another and the sense of his own body. Such a comparison of bodily movements also seems required by simulation theory. Yet this is not knowledge which we have of our own bodily movements or those of others, even as adults. If the basis of the argument is theoretical rather than based on analogy, then the assumption is that we grasp some general relation between types of bodily movements and inner mechanisms. Yet we normally have no account of such movements, except as benevolent or angry, claims which are supposed to form the conclusion of our reasoning and not its starting point.

The epistemological problem of other minds arises from a certain set of assumptions. One is the picture of mental states as inner, directly available only to their subject. A second is an assumption that we can be aware of our own mental states and of the behaviour to which they give rise, while the mentality of others remains in question. The first of these assumptions has been challenged by the account of the embodied nature of subjectivity, which has been offered so far in this book. Our psychological states are constituted out of modes of bodily responsiveness to the world, which are directly observable. Happiness and sadness are written on the faces of ourselves and others. 'The other's consciousness ... is chiefly a certain way of comporting himself towards the world. Thus it is in his conduct, in the manner in which the other deals with the world, that I will be able to discover his consciousness.'[5] In being initiated into our world, we are initiated into recognising the psychological states of others. We learn to recognise them as bodily states, but not as the biologically characterisable movements which form the supposed starting point of folk psychology or the argument from analogy. Bodily behaviour can be read in such a way that its pure physicality disappears, as it were, beneath its significance, as the phonetic characters of words disappear beneath their sense. We learn to be wary of angry people and trustful of benevolent ones. Moreover the kind of knowledge that is involved here is not primarily propositional. It forms rather a kind of practical know-how, which enables us to conduct ourselves appropriately in the presence of others. In Heideggerian terminology, others are ready-to-hand for us. This is not to deny that we are sometimes puzzled, as Lily finds herself in relation to Mrs. Ramsey. It is, however, to see such puzzlement as a question of inter-pretation rather than of hidden certainties. It is more often a question of how we are to conduct ourselves in relation to others than a question of the correctness of our hypotheses about them.

It is not, however, sufficient to counter standard problems of other minds with the view that psychological states are open to view, written on the bodies of others for us to recognise. Such an account leaves unchallenged the suggestion that our own subjectivity could be formed, and we could be aware of it, independently of the subjectivity of such others. In this chapter we will look at the ways in which different continental theorists have challenged this suggestion. In the accounts we are about to explore the subjectivity of others is constitutively linked to the subjectivity of the self. The self is constituted out of its relations to others. For such theorists we could not occupy the starting point of sceptical inquiry, an awareness of our own subjectivity, without accept-ing what sceptics wish to question, namely, the subjectivities of others.

Identification and Mimicry

In his account of 'The Childs's Relation to Others', in *The Primacy of Perception*, Merleau-Ponty uncovers several moments in the child's development, moments which remain in play as aspects of adult identity. He emphasises the importance to early formation of the subject, of the phenomena of imitation, copying the bodily gestures of others, returning a smile with a smile. Here I respond to the actions of another by experiencing them as possibilities for my own body. Following the psychologist Wallon, Merleau-Ponty calls this process 'postural impreg-nation'.[6] It involves a pairing of my body with the body of others. The corporeal schema, or sense of bodily form which enables my own responsiveness to the world, is a schema which is derived from such pairing. At this point the child is unaware of himself and others as separate beings: 'the other's intentions somehow play across my body while my intentions play across his'.[7] This moment of inter-subjectivity also manifests itself by children crying when their peers cry and attributing their actions to others and appropriating the actions of others to themselves. The process which is being described here is unlike either analogy or simulation. In both of those accounts we assume a fixed subjectivity employing strategies to gauge the subjectivities of others. What Merleau-Ponty is drawing attention to, however, is something which makes the formation of such subjectivity possible. The pairing of such comportments towards the world forms our experiences of it. 'It is the attitude of a me which is unaware of itself and lives as easily in others as it does in itself.'[8] Such coupling remains in play in adult life, making possible shared feelings and mutual sympathy as the way in which the world is experienced plays across the bodies of both subjects. 'It is the simple fact that I live in the facial expressions of the other, as I feel him living in mine.'[9]

While our postural schemas are being constituted from such mimicry, the bodies of others are also incorporated into such schemas to form a unified *gestalt*. The removal of the other can then be felt as an incompleteness in one's own body. Here there are analogies with Merleau-Ponty's discussion in earlier texts of the phenomena of phantom limbs. When a limb has been amputated the subject repeatedly responds as if the limb is present, only to be faced each time with the fact of its removal. Within the postural schema, the person's own sense of their bodily form, the limb is still present. Similarly during the formation of subjectivity, and throughout an adult life which such moments inform, the presence of the body of another can be woven into our own sense of our bodily boundaries, so that the loss of that other is experienced as a bodily change. It requires a modification of the imaginary body which constitutes the ego, with all the difficulties which attend such modifications.[10]

Within the psychoanalytic framework the process which most closely approximates to that described by Merleau-Ponty is that of incorporative identification. Identification is characterised by Laplanche and Pontalis as the

> psychological process whereby the subject assimilates an aspect, property, or attribute of the other and is transformed, wholly or partially, after the model the other provides. It is by means of a series of identifications that the personality is constituted and specified.[11]

The series of identifications which serves to form the ego is initially with parents and people in the child's immediate surroundings, but shifts to include figures prominent in their cultural environment and presented within texts or on screen. Identifications remain in place as an ongoing structuring of adult personality. Such identifications are *phantasmatic*. They are not *judgements* of similarity but imaginary assimilations governed by *affect*. Within the psychoanalytic framework the first identifications are seen as being with the mother, but, following the Oedipus complex, Freud and Lacan assume identifications will follow recognition of similarly sexed bodies. Judith Butler, however, stresses that we may identify with a multiplicity of people and images. There need be no prior judgement of similarity. Rather the sense of similarity emerges from the imaginary identification.[12] Such identifications need not be inwardly coherent but yield a complex self, whose different elements remain in tension with each other. For psychoanalysts the process of identification is a psychic process in which the emotional relation to others is placed at the centre of the ongoing formation of the self. This psychic process is given bodily form by the processes of mimesis, which Merleau-Ponty describes.

The Look of Others

In the previous section we have described how ongoing experiences of *sameness* with others serve to constitute the self. Here we will be moving to consider the process by which the self *differentiates itself* from others. This recognition of the 'I' as distinct from both the objects which surround it and from the 'we', is also a moment of self-constitution which necessarily involves other subjects. On both pheno-menological and psychoanalytic accounts the process of differentiation of the self involves the recognition of the 'I' as itself something on which a view can be taken. From about the age of three years, the looks of others can be experienced by the child as irritating or disturbing.[13] They yield a sense of self over and above the corporeal schema, unreflectively informing our intentional negotiations of our environment. In previous chapters we have discussed the role of the mirror image in giving the child a sense of discrete bodily boundaries, and the complexity involved in integrating such an image with the sense of self derived from proprioception. The image which is fed back to the child to initiate this process is not, however, simply that from the mirror. It is an image from other subjects, who the child realises have a view of itself. The view which others have on us is not one which we can have on ourselves. Yet it is a view which needs to be negotiated if we are to recognise ourselves both as an object among objects and one subject among many.

'Following Hegel,' writes Simone de Beauvoir, 'we find in consciousness itself a fundamental hostility towards every other consciousness; the subject can be posed only in being opposed.'[14] The idea that is adopted by both de Beauvoir and Sartre, at least in their best-known texts, is that we are constituted as subjects through *conflict* with others. Hegel's view was that for a subject to recognise herself as a separate subject, with particular desires, she requires recognition from others. In his early work he thought of this recognition as provided by the love of others. But, by the time of *The Phenomenology of Spirit*,[15] the text through which he principally influenced contemporary Continental theorists, he sees the required relation as essentially conflictual. De Beauvoir characterised such conflictual relations in her first novel *She Came to Stay*.[16] Françoise, in this novel, has a relationship with Pierre, which she conceives of as a unity, an idealised immaterial love, in which desires for others are not indulged as they would conflict with their freely chosen unity. Into this world comes Xaviere, the 'incarnation of immediate desire',[17] who comes to desire Pierre to be all hers. In response to this situation Françoise begins an affair with Gerbert to prove the possibility of integrating love and lust. For Xaviere, however, Françoise's affair is an act of revenge for her own relation with Pierre. Moreover, she claims, Françoise is forcing Pierre to stay with her out of guilt. Faced with this picture of herself, Françoise tries to kill Xaviere. 'It is either she or I, it shall be I'.[18] As Toril Moi points out: 'the right to interpret is finally what is at stake'.[19] Françoise is defending her own view of the world and herself.

> Running through Xaviere's manic pleasure, through her hatred and jealousy, the horror exploded, as monstrous and definite as death. In Françoise's face, yet separate from her ... another consciousness was rising ... It was like death ... a total negation.[20]

Sartre develops this account in *Being and Time*, where he famously locates the origins of self-consciousness in the *look* of another: 'I see myself because somebody sees me'.[21] Here Sartre is drawing attention to the fact that it is only in the look of others that I become conscious of being an *object*, something with observable characteristics. Without awareness of the look of others I am aware of myself only as something which has projects and possibilities. Yet, as object, I am an object in another's world, not my own. His spatiality, as Sartre puts it, 'is not my spatiality', 'for instead of a grouping towards me of the objects, there is now an orientation which flees from me'.[22] The becoming aware of myself as an object in another's field of vision is to to be aware of myself and the other as subjects simultaneously, with differing viewpoints onto the world. In the face of such a look, for Sartre, we have two options.

We either make the other an object in their turn or incorporate their viewpoint into our own, 'make an object of the other or assimilate him'.[23] Sartre sees all relationships between particular people as swinging between these two reactions in the process of constituting individual subjectivity.

For Sartre and de Beauvoir the look of others in constituting us as objects in the world threatens our position as subjects, the *pour soi*, whose projects in the world are freely chosen and self-legitimising, for others see us as a something with given sets of characteristics, which yield the behaviour in which we engage. In particular relations the conflict of viewpoints results in each person in the relationship seeking to have her own response to the world recognised by the other as the right one, while demanding – impossibly – that the other concede this freely (as another subject), even if this goes against her own autonomous responses. Freed from its existential preoccupations, however, it becomes less clear that the self/other relations required for self-consciousness, need take a conflictual form. In encountering the look of the other we become aware of ourselves as 'something which can be looked at'. Our body is an object in a common space, which can be observed. As 'something to be looked at' an image is reflected back to us distinct from the pre-reflective corporeal schema informing our engagement with the world. The availability of such an image, and the possibility of our reflecting back to others such an image of themselves, yields a recognition of *different* points of view onto the world. It enables a view of ours as one viewpoint among others, by means of the very process in which we are also given a recognition of ourselves as an inter-subjective object. In the words of one commentator on de Beauvoir:

> I am made aware that I have another self, an objective one which exists only for the Other. My self-for-the-Other is revealed to me as an awareness that the Other has an image of me, as an object in a world whose centre of reference is no longer my consciousness; this experience of being an object entails the Other-as-subject: only another consciousness could cause this decentring of my sense of self.[24]

Although difference is at the heart of this process, it is less clear that it is inevitably conflictual. In the discussion of the child's relation to the mirror image in Chapter 3 we noted that initially the self perceived in the mirror was experienced as 'the self over there',[25] different from the bodily self anchored in sensation. According to Lacan, this latter self was a body experienced in 'bits and pieces'.[26] On the account offered us by Wallon, however, the child does not sacrifice his prior bodily gestalt for an illusory identification with an external image, as Lacan suggests.

Rather the two schemas of the body gradually become integrated. Similarly we can work towards negotiation of the views reflected back to us from others, without requiring the annihilation of such views in order to retain our sense of ourselves as subjects.

In other work of de Beauvoir, and the later work of Sartre, there is a recognition of the possibility of relations with others which, while accepting difference of viewpoints, allows reciprocity. De Beauvoir acknowledges the possibility of others recognising and encouraging each other as sources of meaning. 'It is possible to rise above this conflict if each individual freely recognises the other, each regarding himself and the other simultaneously as object and as subject in a reciprocal manner.'[27] In Sartre's later *Notebooks for an Ethics*, human conflict is no longer seen as necessary: 'once we assume we are both free and an object for others ... there is no longer any ontological reason to remain in the domain of conflict.'[28] He recognises the possibility of a 'love which would involve recognising the aims of the Other, celebrating his world view without attempting to appropriate it, and protecting him with my freedom'.[29]

Woman as Other

De Beauvoir's most famous work moves from the drama of particular relations to make the claim that woman is

> living in a world where men compel her to assume the status of the 'Other'. They propose to stabilise her as object and to doom her to immanence since her transcendence is to be overshadowed and forever transcended by another ego ... which is essential and sovereign.[30]

In this analysis the situation of being the looked at, which informs any encounter with another subject, becomes the general situation of women within society. This is not a situation of women's own making, though they may not be in a position to change it. The position of Other, however, is not simply that of object. Following Hegel, the subject needs recognition by another subject.

> A mere object cannot provide such recognition, and, on the other hand, another subject is likely to attempt to annihilate the first ... so the precarious subject seeks an odd sort of being, one that is fundamentally object, yet enough of a subject that it can perform the function of recognising the subject as subject. Woman is this creature.[31]

For de Beauvoir femininity was the internalisation of this status. In line with her existentialist viewpoint she insisted that women have the capacity to resist such internalisation, transcend their position as Other and reclaim full subjectivity. Nonetheless she also recognises that being able to exercise such a capacity is contingent on the social and material conditions in which people are placed. The conditions of most women constrained the possibility of subjecthood.

> No subject will readily volunteer to become the object ... it is not the Other who, in defining himself as the Other, establishes the One. The Other is posed as such by the One in defining himself as the One. But if the Other is not to regain the status of being the One, he must be submissive enough to accept this alien point of view.[32]

The virtue of her analysis here is to recognise that the inter-subjective relations which are required for subjectivity are mediated by power relations in society at large.

The structure of othering which forms the basis of *The Second Sex* was seen as a general feature of social groups, and not simply applicable to women. In providing her account of it de Beauvoir was influenced by her time in America and contacts with viewpoints of black Americans.

> Thus it is that no group ever sets itself up as the One without at once setting up the Other over against itself. If three travellers chance to occupy the same compartment, that is enough to make vaguely hostile 'others' out of all the rest of the passengers on the train ... to the native of a country all who inhabit other countries are 'foreigners'; Jews are 'different' for the anti-Semite, Negroes are 'inferior' for American racists; aborigines are 'natives' for colonists; proletarians are the 'lower class' for the privileged.[33]

The most famous application of this structure to colonialism is found in Fanon's *Black Skin, White Masks*. 'The real Other for the white man is and will continue to be the black man', 'for not only must the black man be black; he must be black in relation to the white man'.[34] The way in which the black man is othered, for Fanon, has some differences from the account of women given by de Beauvoir. For Fanon the black man is viewed simply as an object, a 'crushing objecthood'.[35] He does not occupy the in-between status which enables women a semblance of subjectivity, in order to allow them to provide recognition for men. In contrast, for the colonisers, the colonised are denied any possibility of occupying the position of 'the one who looks' and thereby any recognition of subjecthood. 'Fanon finds himself ... simply an object in the midst of other objects'.[36]

In his analysis of this process of Othering, Fanon also adds, to the existentialist notion of otherness, resources from psychoanalysis. The Othering of blackness makes the black body the bearer of repressed phantasy and desire. What is created is an imaginary other body,[37] which exemplifies the aspects of self which cannot be accepted. These, as part of the imagined black body, serve to secure a sense of an exemplary white self. This imagined Other therefore has its origin in the One. It is a construct to secure the selfhood of the One.

The importance of the accounts offered by de Beauvoir and Fanon is that they make it clear that, in the existentialist story of self/other relations, not all subjects are equal. Differences in social power relations mediate the chances of establishing subjectivity through the mediated encounters with the subjectivity of others. De Beauvoir and Fanon both call for an ethics of 'reciprocal recognitions', a reversal of polarities by a process of intersubjectivity. What such a process would involve is the reclaiming of a subjectivity, which is distinct from an internalisation of the view reflected back from the dominant group. It also requires the construction of a view onto that dominant group. Consequently these differing viewpoints between such subject/objects require negotiation. Both writers, however, recognise that the prospect of such reciprocity requires changes in social structures.

Language as Other

As we have seen in discussing the work of Lacan the subject is initially undifferentiated from a union with the mother. It moves towards recognition of itself by means of a series of identifications with others and with images reflected back by others and with the image of itself in a mirror. However, for Lacan, in the next stage of the process of subject formation, the Other, by means of which our own status as subjects is achieved, is not, as for phenomenologists, other subjects, but the impersonal structure of language. In his account of this process Lacan moves away from phenomenology and towards structuralism. The subject becomes an 'effect of an autonomous symbolic syntax, engendered by the structure of language, the "signifying chain" as he calls it.'[38] For Lacan it is the Other of language which subdues and objectifies the subject, at the same time as making a space for her as a subject. This language constitutes a system, a pre-established linguistic universe, a positioning within which provides the possibility of subjecthood. Paradoxically, for Lacan, such an entry into the Symbolic also involves a 'fading of the subject'.[39] The positioning in the symbolic involves a loss of the imaginary world and a split in the subject, as the imaginary identifications become unavailable to articulation. The subject can identify herself only through the signifier which she employs, a signifier which signals a position within an objective linguistic structure. The subject therefore fades at the very moment at which she makes herself an intelligible subject of speech and action. She is 'split' between that aspect which is captured and objectified by the signifier she employs for herself and that which eludes it. Yet even the latter is only manifest in other, non-standard signifiers.

'Man, woman, they are only signifiers. It is from that, from speech in its incarnation as one sex or the other, that they derive their function.'[40] Within this framework, the structure of othering, of which Fanon and de Beauvoir provided a phenomenological account, is itself a feature of linguistic structure. Language works by the assignment of a privileged term, in opposition to which another term is defined. Sense is generated internally to the system of language by a series of 'binary oppositions'. Each term is defined by its position in the system, in relation to its opposition to other terms. We become formed in language as the occupier of a privileged position, or as lacking it. To resist such signification is to become unintelligible, unable to communicate or to act. Hence the colonisers are simply forming themselves and others in terms of a discourse already laid out for them. Our communication with others requires that we both occupy a position within a symbolic order, whose content is a matter of impersonal regulation.

Here we have lost the phenomenological account of a subjectivity as a perspective onto a world, individuated by its engagements with other and different subjectivities. In its place we have distinctions between different bodies in terms of the signifiers in the texts associated with them. Such a conception also runs through much poststructuralist thought. Derrida shares with Lacan a conception of subjectivity as constituted by language. He thinks of language, however, not simply as a system of differences, but as constituted by the 'movement of différance'. It is marked by the operation of iterability.[41] Future uses of a linguistic term retain traces of its past uses, which nonetheless fail to fix its meaning in a determinate fashion. Derrida remarks 'this movement of différance does not happen to a transcendental subject. It produces it',[42] so that 'subjectivity is ... an effect of différance, an effect inscribed in a system of différance'.[43] That is to say, the subject is not to be thought of as a user of language, through whose fixed resources she can convey her thoughts. Rather she acquires her subject status through the indeterminacy that her linguistic (and other) acts over time imply. Derrida's view of subjectivity is then that it is not, as it were, a fixed point, from which the world is viewed – as the metaphor of perspective implies – but a shifting collection of signifiers, of which no fixed sense can be made. The language we utter, like other bits of bodily behaviour, is not expressions of consciousness, but texts whose significance depends on their context and connections, a matter of public reading.

Is there any way of marrying the poststructuralist insight that subjects constitute texts, whose meaning is subject to the workings of iterability, with the phenomenologists' picture of particular subjects whose individuation required encounters with other particular subjectivities? To do this we have to replace a conception of iterability as the mutations of an objective linguistic structure with a recognition that the meanings that form individual subjectivities emerge from the readings which one (or more) subjects provide of another (or more). The interpretation of subjects as texts requires other subjectivities whose reading and responses are necessary for something to count as a text with meaning at all. In Derrida's words there is no relation to oneself 'that is not forced to defer itself by passing through the other ... who is supposed to send his signature back to me'.[44] In insisting on this form of inter-subjectivity we do not need to assume subjectivities prior to the possibility of mutual readings, who then undertake such readings. They can, rather, become formed by the process itself. Neither do we have to abandon recognition of a certain publicness, a degree of anonymity in the meanings which are assigned. Their appropriateness requires the possibility of other similarly placed readers coming up with similar reading responses.

Here we might be reminded of Wittgenstein's recognition that what makes a certain state count as, for example, pain is the responses of others to its expression. In the words of one commentator:

> On this approach, the behaviour of a living thing is not a scene as of, say, 'a subject experiencing pain', except in its structural relation to a reading-response – even if the 'subject' is, in fact, isolated, and even if it is, in fact, 'oneself' who is in pain.[45]

The range of such responses yields the contours of the pain itself, but they only do so if they are responses of bodies whose own expressions could be given meaning in the same way. The recognition of behaviour as pain behaviour requires creatures with a certain range of responses. It is on this that the interdependence of subjectivity on inter-subjectivity rests. Insistence on such inter-subjectivity does not dispense with the workings of iterability. Both the temporal dimension of meaning and the consequent indeterminacy of the meanings attributed remain firmly in play.

Alterity and the Ethical Demands of the Face

It would be a mistake to conclude from the discussion above that the dependence of subjectivity on inter-subjectivity invokes some ideal of mutual transparency. We have seen in the discussion in our previous chapter that Derrida was critical of any such aspiration. For him our encounters with others were marked by an awareness of moments of unbridgeable difference, radical otherness. For Derrida there is no possibility of fully inscribing the reality of the Other. He writes in *Postcards*, 'sometimes I tell myself that you are my love; then it is only my love, I tell myself interpellating myself thus ... But I also know ... that you are well beyond what I repeat as "my love", living, living, living',[46] and 'the post ... begins with a destination without address ... There is no destination. The condition for me ... is that you are there, over there quite alive outside me. Out of reach. And that you send me back'.[47] In his discussions with Levinas (see below), he claims, 'the understanding of being always concerns alterity, and par excellence the alterity of the Other in all its originality'.[48] For Derrida it is the 'thereness' of the Other that keeps her as Other, something beyond inscription or imaginary embodiments. Drucilla Cornell comments: 'this "thereness" of the Other also demands the recognition of the singularity of her being ... her uniqueness, her singularity'.[49] For Derrida recognition of such alterity is pivotal in the formation of the ethical relation.

Here Derrida's thought is very close to that of Emmanuel Levinas. In *Totality and Infinity* Levinas invokes our experiencing *the face* of another as the way in which we confront exteriority, the 'void that breaks the totality can be maintained against an inevitably totalising and synoptic thought only if thought finds itself *faced* with an other, refractory to categories'.[50] The other person who faces me confronts me with an excessiveness, which cannot be captured within any of the concepts which I might employ. Central to Levinas's thought here is his reference to *the face*: 'The way in which the other presents himself exceeding *the idea of the other in me*, we here name face'.[51] The face of the other, as Levinas uses it here, is something beyond its surface physiognomy. It summons us to recognition of a radical otherness and demands an ethical response, 'a command which calls a halt to the availability of consciousness'.[52] The demand which is made by the face of the other is received passively. We are unable to appropriate or direct it. Here the face interrupts the everyday existence of the subject confronting it, but not, as in Sartre, as a second consciousness struggling to assert dominance, but as something making a call on us. Despite the way the face demands a response it 'does not limit but promotes my freedom by arousing my goodness'.[53] That the face elicits the reaction it does is a precondition of my activity having an a ethical character, of its being activity for which one is held responsible by others, which is the point of freedom. To recognise the neediness of the other is not to represent it under categories, but to discover oneself as responsible. For

Levinas, such responsibility is infinite and asymmetrical. I am responsible without waiting for the other to be responsible in return.

The cardinal ethical sin in the writings of both Derrida and Levinas is the refusal to recognise the otherness of the other, instead reducing them to a position in 'the logic of the same'; a position within the categories which form our own interpretation of the world. It is somewhat ironic that for both theorists such an appropriation seems to have taken place with their use of the category 'woman'. In common with a recurrring motif in continental thought, the 'feminine' comes to stand, particularly in Levinas's early writings, 'not merely as a quality different from the masculine, but as "the very quality of difference", in such a way that alterity seemed to be the positive meaning and content of the feminine'.[54] (This was attacked by de Beauvoir in the *Second Sex*.) Later Levinas relies on the image of the pregnant woman who gives over her body to her son, to capture the ethical relation of responsibility. In both these uses, in different ways, the content of woman has been appropriated to fill a position within masculine discourse. This is a continuation of a use of the feminine, which Derrida criticised in Lacan. In the Lacanian symbolic woman is simply what is not man. Her position is articulated purely in relation to that of man. In Irigaray's terms woman is 'the other of the same'.[55] For Derrida such a foreclosure on the meaning of woman is to deny her genuine alterity, one beyond the masculine symbolic. The refusal to contain 'woman' or any other within the categories of our own making is, for Derrida, the crucial moment in the ethical relation. Nonetheless Derrida himself does not always avoid this trap. Frequently the metaphor of femininity or woman is used in his writings as a metaphor for otherness itself, or for the indeterminacy of that which escapes fixity.

Levinas, in rejecting a 'totalising' conception of understanding, sees no understanding of the Other as adequate, or ethically acceptable, which conceptualises them within a system, for example, within a framework of psychological theory. For this will, in Hegelian fashion, impose our own view of the world upon them, locating them within that world, rather than responding to them as a voice from beyond it. The alternative is not to capitulate to the Other's view. It is rather to respond to the Other as making demands *prior to any specific view of the world*. For Levinas, in contrast to Heidegger, such relationships are prior to our having a world, prior to ontology and consequently psychology. For Heidegger, as we have noted, the experience of others comes primarily in dealing with things ready to hand as, for instance, 'the field ... belonging to such and such a person ... the book ... bought at So and so's shop'.[56] That is to say that it involves experiences which reveal the world for the subject as necessarily a shared world. In contrast to such a generalised *being with* subjects, Levinas takes as prior the relationship to particular others, as subjects making demands on us. On one account other subjects are part of a collective 'we' among whom we find ourselves. On the alternative picture particular others call us to an exteriority beyond our world. The account which Levinas is offering us here is not simply that of the precondition for ethical responsiveness. The recognition of the face, as making demands on us, is what constitutes our own subjectivity. In line with the other accounts discussed above, recognition of others forms us as subjects. What is distinctive for Levinas is that it is the alterity of others, their radical otherness, which plays this role, together with the demand which that makes on me.

Summary

This chapter has identified different moments in the formation of subjectivity and revealed how, at each of these moments, subjectivity is constitutively linked to inter-subjectivity. Our own selves are ontologically dependent on other selves, to whom we stand in particular relations. The moments, which have sometimes been discussed here in developmental terms, capture aspects of selfhood, all of which remain in play in adult life. The identifications with others, the weaving of others into our bodily gestalt, the response to the look of others, the positioning of ourselves and others within language, and the recognition of radical difference are aspects of our everyday living alongside others which makes our own formation as subjects possible.

Notes

1. M. Heidegger, *Being and Time*, trans. J. Maquarrie and E. Robinson (Oxford: Blackwell, 1967), H 129.
2. Ibid., H 118.
3. V. Woolf, *To the Lighthouse* (London: Granada, 1977), pp. 50–1.
4. M. Merleau-Ponty, 'The Child's Relations with Others', in M. Merleau-Ponty, *The Primacy of Perception and Other Essays on Phenomenological Psychology* (Evanston, IL: Northwestern University Press, 1964), p. 115.
5. Ibid., p. 117.
6. Ibid., p. 118.
7. Ibid., p. 119.
8. Ibid., p. 119.
9. Ibid., p. 146.
10. See the discussion of the Imaginary Body in Chapter 3 above. The integration of others into our bodily schemas helps explain why the loss of someone close to us is

felt as a change in our own bodies, leaving us constantly reaching out to a point that is no longer occupied.

11. J. Laplanche and J.-B. Pontalis, *The Language of Psychoanalysis* (London: Karnac Books, 1973), p. 205.
12. J. Butler, 'Phantasmatic Identification and the Assumption of Sex', in J. Butler, *Bodies That Matter* (New York and London: Routledge, 1993).
13. Merleau-Ponty, *Primacy of Perception*, p. 153.
14. S. de Beauvoir, *The Second Sex* (London: Penguin, 1972), p. 17.
15. G. W. F. Hegel, *The Phenomenology of Spirit* (Oxford: Clarendon Press, 1977).
16. S. de Beauvoir, *She Came to Stay*, trans. Y. Moyse and R. Senhouse (London: Flamingo, 1984); discussed by E. Holveck, 'Simone de Beauvoir's Desire to Express La joie d'exister', in H. Silverman (ed.), *Philosophy and Desire* (New York and London: Routledge, 2000).
17. Holveck, 'Simone de Beauvoir's Desire to Express La joie d'exister', p. 99.
18. Ibid., p. 101.
19. Ibid., p. 103, quoting T. Moi, *Simone de Beauvoir: The Making of an Intellectual Woman* (Oxford: Blackwell, 1994), p. 122.
20. Holveck, 'Simone de Beauvoir's Desire to Express La joie d'exister', p. 104; De Beauvoir, *She Came to Stay*, p. 291.
21. J.-P. Sartre, *Being and Nothingness*, trans. H. Barnes (London: Methuen, 1969), p. 260.
22. Ibid., p. 255.
23. Ibid., p. 363.
24. K. and E. Fullbrook, 'Simone de Beauvoir', in S. Critchley and W. R. Schroeder (eds), *A Companion to Continental Philosophy* (Malden, MA: Blackwell, 1998), p. 275.
25. Merleau-Ponty, *Primacy of Perception*, pp. 128–9.
26. J. Lacan, 'Some Reflections on the Ego', *International Journal of Psychoanalysis*, 34, 1953.
27. De Beauvoir, *Second Sex*, p. 172.
28. J.-P. Sartre, *Cahiers pour une morale* (Paris: Gallimard, 1983), p. 26, quoted in C. Howells, 'Sartre and Levinas', in R. Bernasconi and D. Wood (eds), *The Provocation of Levinas* (London and New York: Routledge, 1988).
29. Howells, 'Sartre and Levinas', p. 97.
30. De Beauvoir, *Second Sex*, p. 172.
31. M. B. Mader and K. Oliver, 'French Feminism', in R. Solomon and D. Sherman (eds), *The Blackwell Guide to Continental Philosophy* (Oxford: Blackwell, 2003), p. 31.
32. De Beauvoir, *Second Sex*, p. 17.
33. Ibid., pp. 16–17.
34. F. Fanon, *Black Skins, White Masks*, trans C. L. Markman (New York: Grove Press, 1967), p. 110; quoted in D. Fuss, *Identification Papers* (New York and London: Routledge, 1995), p. 142.
35. Fuss, *Identification Papers*, p. 143.
36. Ibid., p. 143.
37. See the discussion of the Imaginary Body in Chapter 3.
38. See E. Wright (ed.), *Feminism and Psychoanalysis* (Oxford: Blackwell, 1992), entry 'Other/other', p. 298.
39. J. Lacan, *The Four Fundamental Concepts of Psychoanalysis* (Harmondsworth: Penguin, 1979), p. 208.

40. J. Lacan, *Le Seminaire* (Paris: Encore, 1975), book 20, pp. 39–40.
41. See further discussion of iterability in Chapter 6, above.
42. Quoted in M. Frank, 'Is Self Consciousness presence à soi?', in D. Wood (ed.), *Derrida: A Critical Reader* (Oxford: Blackwell, 1992), p. 229.
43. Ibid., p. 227.
44. J. Derrida, *Otobiographies: The Ear of the Other*, trans. A. Ronell (Lincoln, NE: University of Nebraska Press, 1985), p. 88, quoted in S. Glendinning, *On Being with Others* (London: Routledge, 1998), p. 146.
45. Glendinning, *On Being with Others*, p. 147.
46. Quoted in D. Cornell, 'Where Love Begins', in E. K. Feder, M. Rawlinson and E. Zakin (eds), *Derrida and Feminism* (London: Routledge, 1997), pp. 197–8.
47. Ibid.
48. Ibid., p. 199.
49. Ibid.
50. E. Levinas, *Totality and Infinity* (Pittsburgh: Duquesue University Press, 1969), p. 40.
51. Ibid., p. 50.
52. E. Levinas, 'The Trace of the Other', in W. McNeill and K. S. Feldman (eds), *Continental Philosophy: An Anthology* (Oxford: Blackwell, 1998), p. 181.
53. Levinas, *Totality and Infinity*, p. 200.
54. D. Perpich, 'Philosophy of the Other: Levinas', in S. Glendinning (ed.), *The Edinburgh Encyclopedia of Continental Philosophy* (Edinburgh: Edinburgh University Press, 1999), p. 607.
55. L. Irigaray, 'Equality and Difference', in M. Whitford (ed.), *The Irigaray Reader* (Oxford: Blackwell, 1991).
56. Heidegger, *Being and Time*, H 118.

Index